THE
ASTROLOGER'S
NODE
BOOK

THE ASTROLOGER'S NODE BOOK

Donna Van Toen

SAMUEL WEISER, INC.

York Beach, Maine

First published in 1981 by
Samuel Weiser, Inc.
York Beach, Maine 03910

Fourth printing, 1992

Library of Congress Card Number: 82-114845

ISBN 0-87728-521-7
CCP

Printed in the United States of America.

The paper used in this publication meets the minimum
requirements of the American National Standard for
Permanence of Paper for Printed Library Materials
Z39.48-1984.

Contents

Acknowledgments

To Debbie Richardson, Suzanne Labreche, Mary Van Toen and my many students whose assistance made this book a reality.

With special thanks to Charlie for his encouragement, understanding, and patience.

Why This Book Was Written

My first encounter with the lunar nodes was in a textbook. "The lunar nodes are very important," I read. Why, they didn't say. References were made to luck, evolution and karma but concrete definitions were sadly lacking.

Intrigued, I began searching through other texts to find meaningful interpretations of the nodes. Some of what I found seemed to be mere whimsy. Some interpretations sounded logical but didn't work in practice. A few books—particularly Bernice Grebner's *Lunar Nodes—New Concepts* struck a responsive chord, making me believe that the nodes were indeed "very important". I began at this point to pay close attention to the nodal positions in the charts I did and as a result I began to formulate some theories of my own, which I initially kept to myself.

However, in teaching beginners, I found that they too found the present literature on the nodes to be lacking. They demanded more than what the books gave them. At this point I offered my own findings which my students found useful and accurate.

I hope that you, like my students, will find this material useful. I don't claim that the material presented here is the ultimate in knowledge on lunar nodes, nor do I claim that my theories are the only right ones. What works for me, what works for my students, may not work for you. Since I'm a practicing astrologer rather than a researcher I readily admit that in my enthusiasm to find something that works I may have overlooked information that was for one reason or another unavailable to me.

Use this information, but don't take it as absolute for this book is merely a starting point. If it enhances your understanding of the nodes, great. If it encourages you to formulate your own theories, so much the better. But don't let it be "enough". We have much to learn yet.

What are the Moon's Nodes?

The Moon's nodes are imaginary points that mark off a sort of celestial equator. They're used by astronomers in the calculation of astronomical distances, eclipses and other important data.

Since the Moon's nodes aren't planets, it may seem hard to believe that they have any place in the horoscope. But they have as much place as the Part of Fortune or the ascendant, neither of which are planets. Like these points, the nodes are measures of the relationship between time and space. In other words, they show where you're at as of your birth time.

Although I've read nothing about how the nodes came to be used by astrologers, it seems likely that they were used in calculating the timing of eclipses, since the eclipse has traditionally been thought to herald momentous change on both mundane and personal levels.

Traditionally, the nodes were referred to as the Dragon's Head (north node) and the Dragon's Tail (south node), with the north node representing nourishment and the south node representing excrement. The nodes are symbolized thusly: ☊ (north node) and ☋ (south node) maybe representing a dragon's head and tail. Personally, I find the symbols confusing and have chosen to designate them with a simple NN and SN. If you find the intrinsic meditational value of the traditional symbols worthwhile, there's no reason for you to adopt the simpler notation. On the other hand, if you get confused by them, there's no need to run the risk of getting them mixed up with each other.

Calculation of nodal positions is a simple process. All decent ephemerides list their daily positions, which can then be adjusted by using diurnals or logs in the same way you adjust other planetary positions for the correct birth time. Some ephemerides give positions for both the mean (estimated) position and true position. You might want to experiment with both positions and see what differences show up.

Ephemerides list only the position for the north node. That's because the south node is always directly opposite the north node. The nodes are always in exact opposition. Here we have our first clue to the interpretation of the nodes. The opposition is the proverbial "tug-of-war" aspect. In opposition, two conflicting factors are tugging at you, demanding your attention. There are several ways you can resolve the conflict. You can sacrifice one factor at another's expense. You can let the stronger factor prevail until the weaker factor develops strength enough to cause you to switch alliances. You can try to effect some sort of compromise, or you can hang in there and let the two factors pull you to bits. This last solution seems a bit self-defeating but judging from the number of people who suffer from stress-related diseases, mental breakdown, various types of addiction, etc., it's one that many people consciously or unconsciously choose.

The oppositon transcends the vertical and horizontal axes of the horoscope. Therefore, the conflict of the nodes takes on tones of me vs. us, independence vs. dependence, fulfilling your own needs in your own way vs. fulfilling your needs in a publicly acceptable but possibly less satisfying way. Your solution to the conflict will depend then on your psychological make-up (as shown by your chart), your conditioning (parents, peers, schools etc.), and your level of self-awareness (how well you know your needs).

If you look through your ephemeris, you'll notice that the nodes are moving almost constantly in a retrograde motion. Now retrograde implies two things. First of all it's synonymous with inner or subconcious energies, which means that if you're not in touch with your gut-level responses to things you can have difficulty understanding the source of your conflict. Secondly, retrogrades frequently symbolize events that occur before you have the maturity to understand them. Childhood traumas of various types are good examples. These needn't be major traumas like being abused. In fact, just as often they involve rather trivial but still threatening experiences—having to do with not having what "everybody else" has, for example, even if that particular thing happens to be useless or downright harmful. So quite often, badly-balanced nodes give a feeling that something's wrong or lacking or just a little weird, but you can't quite put your finger on what it is or why it's a problem.

It should be mentioned that there are instances when the nodes are direct and instances when they're also stationary. It's interesting to speculate on how this affects interpretation. Would they, like direct planets, work more overtly when direct? Or, since retrogression is the rule rather than the exception, would this create further difficulties? My own limited research in this area is too sketchy to draw from but perhaps some other dedicated student will explore this area.

Some Theories on Nodal Meanings

As in many other areas of astrology, astrologers have differing opinions as to the values and meanings of the nodes. Before dismissing them, we should touch on these theories and try to determine what value they might have.

1. The nodes are just more meaningless clutter.

The main proponents of this theory seem to fall into two categories—disgruntled students and purists. The students have generally adopted this theory after failing to find any value in available interpretations. Sometimes they change opinions after coming into contact with new literature.

The purists are a little harder to peg. Many astrologers of this type are ultra-conservative. They eschew not only the nodes but also midpoints, Arabian Parts, and hypothetical planets. Their reasoning is that if astrology is ever to be accepted by the scientific community, it has to be on the basis of proven data, rather than coincidence. Thus they work solely with planetary influences and ignore anything that's not a planet, angle or sign.

Although it's true that any hypothetical planet or point should be viewed with healthy skepticism, I think that the fact that the nodes have been in use since antiquity makes them deserving of at least a little attention. It's also interesting to note that Hindu astrologers—many of whom are so conservative that they still don't use the discovered outer planets in their work—unfailingly use the nodes. Granted, that doesn't prove anything, but it should at least make you wonder why.

2. The nodes show past and future karma.

This theory states that the south node represents karma from past lives while the north node represents dharma, or future karma. Another offshoot of this theory is one that states that the north node represents those qualities which you've neglected to develop while the south node represents what you've developed instead. There's probably a grain of truth in this—especially in the latter statement. However, it's been my experience to find that anything that's not clearly understood quite often gets neatly filed away under the karmic catchall, the assumption being that if we truly understood the implications of life experiences on this plane we wouldn't have to be here. Result: Karma becomes a neat crutch for what we can't or won't understand about ourselves and our lives.

Before you decide that I'm aspiritual or obviously un-evolved, let me state here and now that I definitely believe there's a purpose for our being here and that many of us have lived before and some will live again. But the theory of karma can be a dangerous one if it's accompanied by a lack of common sense or a lack of solid understanding of metaphysical principles. I've heard students say things like, "I can't help being bossy, it's because I was bossed around so much in my past life." I have also heard clients say, "Madame Oldsoul says my health problems are karmic retribution for vanity in a past life." Now maybe Student was really a slave in a past life and maybe Client was Snow White's wicked stepmother. In any case, it's over and done with and justifying rudeness or accepting suffering unquestionably isn't going to do anything to improve the quality of your present life. To me, karma isn't an evolutionary tic-tac-toe game. Nor is it an enforced life sentence of suffering. Karma is a promise to pay for what you get. It's responsibility for your actions. An excuse for reprehensible behavior it's not; nor is it an excuse to neglect your physical, material or emotional well-being. So if you're looking at this theory to explain why you're a compulsive eater, or on welfare, or stuck in a miserable marriage you're probably not looking closely enough or deeply enough at the real significance of the nodes. The Moon's nodes may have something to do with where you're at right now. If you don't want to be where you are, you owe it to yourself to change your situation instead of making yourself and those around you miserable.

3. The nodes show how you relate to your environment.

Probably they will. Many astrologers say that the north node shows where you're in tune with current trends and the south node shows where you're out of step. Thus they have some influence on both popularity and ability to take advantage of opportunities. I've found cases where this is very valid.

4. The nodes represent points of good luck and bad luck.

In this theory, the north node becomes a good luck charm and the south node becomes a sort of perpetual jinx. This theory can work, but it often works in reverse and sometimes doesn't work at all. Personally, I think it's a bit oversimplified, for reasons I'll explain later.

So how do you go about interpreting the nodes? Well, first you consider the material we covered in Chapter 2. Next, you come to terms with what the nodes represent. To me, the north node is a point of growth, a point of untapped potential. This potential is invariably very positive, yet the north node is seldom what you'd instantly recognize as an area where fate smiles on you. Good luck implies having things come easily to you. This isn't usually the case with the north node. To get at this potential you have to work darned hard. If you do this you may eventually discover yourself having very nice things happen to you. But it's not merely luck—you've worked to earn them, whether consciously or unconsciously.

In contrast to the north node, the south node represents a point of stagnation. Here we find the potentials that keep you from growing. This is where you do what comes naturally, where you take the line of least resistance. Now the qualities the south node represents may not actually be vices, but chances are that you've over-exploited them at the expense of your north node potentials.

Let's take an example. Suppose you have south node in Libra. This means that you could very well find it easier to grin and bear things you don't like instead of standing up and stating your feelings. What's the problem? You're too agreeable. Chances are that nobody's going to fault you for trying to get along with those you come in contact with, but chances are also good that there'll be people who impose upon your amiability. Sure, they've got problems or they wouldn't do it. But if you don't stick up for yourself, *you're* going to have problems. So what do you do? You tap your Aries' north node assertiveness potential. Initially, no doubt, you'll feel like a real meanie refusing to let all those so-called friends step on you. And you may occasionally overcompensate for your past easygoingness by getting quite aggressively vehement. But eventually you'll get your nodes balanced and will find your problems either greatly alleviated or totally solved.

On the other hand, you can decide that assertiveness isn't something you want to develop. In that case, the north node potential remains untapped, and you're forced to exploit your south node. The more you do this, the more likely it is that you'll experience a kind of vague dissatisfaction with your lot in life. Why? Because subconsciously you know something's missing.

The following chapters are designed to help you determine how well you've balanced your nodes and how to find that missing part and develop it if necessary, or how to keep your nodes balanced if you've been successful so far.

Nodal Signs and the Yeah-But Dialogues

No doubt you've had the misfortune to be ensnared at least once by a practitioner of the art of yeah-butting. This person is one of the ultimate time wasters, a royal pain guaranteed to cast a shadow on even the most optimistic outlook. His or her usual modus operandi is to approach you with a problem, seemingly seeking your advice. The conversation usually goes something like this:

Yeah-But: I'm having a real problem losing weight. Tell me, how do you manage to stay so slim?

You : I watch what I eat and I exercise.

Yeah-But: Exercise? What sort of exercise?

You : Mainly walking.

Yeah-But Really? I love walking. I walk all the time, but it doesn't seem to help.

You : That's too bad.

Yeah-But: Yeah, I wish there was something else I could do.

You : Well, there's the Yoga class at the Y...

Yeah-But: Forget that—I just can't hack all those pseudo-spiritual types.

You : Well, there's a lot of other things—bicycling, dancing, swimming.

Yeah-But: Yeah, but I can't afford a bicycle right now and I'm so fat that I feel out of place at the discos. And swimming is out—I never learned how. I've got a terrible fear of the water you know.

You : Maybe you should try a diet. Weight Watchers is good.

16

Yeah-But: Yeah, but they meet on Mondays and I'd have to give up my bridge club. I couldn't desert them now—they'd be short a person.

You   : Maybe you should get a doctor to put you on a diet then.

Yeah-But: Maybe...But I don't think a diet is the answer. I have to eat out a lot and you just can't refuse things when people go to all the trouble of cooking them for you.

You   : Why not? Real friends would understand. I bet they'd even go out of their way to cooperate.

Yeah-But: Yeah, but . . . Hey, look at the time. If I don't hurry I won't have time for supper before the movie tonight . . . Say, could you call me a cab?

As Yeah-But plunks himself or herself into a cab for the two-block journey home, you may feel anything from disappointment to frustration to anger. Yeah-But has just successfully wasted your time and made you feel like an idiot. By negating your every suggestion, he or she has subtly suggested that your opinions are really not worth much. Furthermore, in trying to help, you've been tricked into giving Yeah-But an opportunity to "prove" that he or she is really concerned about self-improvement but is "trapped" by a set of inextricable circumstances. And you wonder why you feel blah? Wonder no more—just don't get conned again!

Nobody enjoys a Yeah-But. Yet we are all Yeah-Buts at one time or another, consciously or unconsciously. And our most likely sources of Yeah-But dialogues are frequently found by taking a look at our nodes. In these astrological Yeah-But dialogues, the north node generally offers you advice of some sort or tells you something you must do to become happier, healthier or more alive. The advice or statement is valid but threatening—either because it sounds like too much work for uncertain results or because it reminds you consciously or unconsciously of past failures or traumas.

Following are some typical manifestations of the Yeah-But syndrome, along with possible causes and possible solutions. I've also included typical manifestations of what I call

unbalanced nodes. Of course there are other ways these imbalances can work out, and if you have basic working
knowledge of the sign polarities, you should have no trouble
adding several of your own observations to each of mine.

A word should be said about the solutions given. These,
from my experiences as an astrologer seem to be the most frequently chosen methods of coping in each case. I have listed
them impartially. Some will make sense to you; others won't.
For every problem, there's a good solution and a bad one. Furthermore, what's perfect for you may be a horrible solution for
someone else.

Aries North Node

You need to learn to do things for yourself.

Libra South Node

Yeah, but it's much easier to let others do things for me.
Every time I try to do my own thing either somebody takes advantage of me or I wind up getting somebody mad at me.

Major problem

You're not rational when it comes to relationships.

Possible reasons

You have such a hang-up about being fair to everybody
that you bend over backwards for others at the sake of your
own individuality. You've stifled your leadership abilities
because using them led to friction or discord. You're unable to
get started on things without help due to lack of ambition or
self-motivation. Life experiences have over-emphasized the
value of leaning on others and encouraged passivity as a
means of gaining acceptance.

Possible solutions

Force yourself to undertake leadership roles. Dare to be
enthusiastic about your beliefs and interests. Cultivate spon-
taneity. Do things on your own once in a while. Find a guru to
follow. Find a big strong man (or good woman) to lean on.

Observation

With Libra south node, decision-making is often a problem. This is because with Libra south node, there's a tendency

to overdevelop logic to the point that it smothers the Aries feeling and acting functions. However, feelings can't be totally ignored. They have a way of coming out and moving you in certain directions whether you choose to be aware of them or not. If they're denied positive expression through individuality and assertiveness, they'll be forced to take a negative route through insincerity, meddling or dependence. With Libra south node, rationalization can lead to irrationality, since feelings get lost in the shuffle. Usually, this dependency on passive intellectualizing is the result of some traumatic experience where feelings have let the individual down. Often he or she has been ridiculed or rejected for reasons that were never clearly understood and from that point on has decided that feelings can't be trusted. So figuring out strategies replaces feelings. The Libran south noder takes great pains to be sure that all decisions about marriage, job and life style in general are formulated logically and planned thoroughly. The trouble is that logic without feeling leads to marriage without love, prestige without satisfaction, and existence without living. Eventually depression sets in and logic ceases to function. At that point, Libra south node is forced to get in touch with his or her feelings and take appropriate action, thus attaining a nodal balance between Aries and Libra.

In my experience, the person with an over-developed Libra south node:

- Dislikes being alone
- Asks for help and advice but then seems almost resentful of it
- Spends a great deal of time and money on grooming, cosmetics, clothing etc.
- Speaks in a monotone or a very tiny voice
- Is indecisive
- Is extremely cooperative to the point of being a door mat
- Has an inferiority complex
- Is a gracious host or hostess whose door is invariably open to everyone at all times
- Works hard at romance
- Feels sorry for single people, regardless of their circumstances

Taurus North Node

You have real hang-ups about earnings and resources.

Scorpio South Node

Yeah, but that's because I've been ripped off so often. You just can't trust people.

Problem

You haven't built up your own resources.

Possible Reasons

You don't really know what you want. You resent other people's personal or material successes. You have sexual misconceptions or misconceptions about material wealth. Maybe you were brought up to equate affection and caring with getting material things. On rare occasions people with south node in Scorpio have a "you've got to be more crooked to make any money in this world" philosophy. More often, there's a tendency to make changes just for the sake of changing.

Possible solutions

Learn to enjoy both giving and receiving whether the exchange involves affection, compliments, money or whatever. Develop a strong sense of personal values based on your own needs. Forget about morals and do what you have to do.

Observation

Taurus north node generally has to be taught to value money and material goods. There's often some sort of hang-up about the actual process of working—a dislike of any type of menial or manual labor, a refusal to prove your worth, an insistence on starting at the top, etc. Sometimes there's actually a contempt for money; other times money is OK as long as you don't have to have the hassle of working for it. Occasionally there's a "gimme" fixation, while at other times there's a "take-it" fixation. Sometimes there's an over-emphasis on sexual resources. And I've seen a few cases where total resources were invested in other-worldly pursuits—contacting the dead, attaining trance states, researching various paths leading towards spiritual evolution, etc. Taurus north node has a hard time seeing the connection between development of his or her personal and material resources and being able to successfully relate to others and to the material world in general. Depending on the overall chart, he or she takes a stance of total giving or total taking. Many Taurus north noders concentrate on one resource exclusively to the detriment of others so that time, money, sex, etc. becomes the only means of barter available to them. When this resource is depleted they no longer have anything to fall back on and must either work to develop other resources or become totally dependent on others. Taurus north node also seems to be quite common in people who have suffered material, educational, or emotional deprivations in childhood.

The person with an over-developed Scorpio south node:
- Consciously or unconsciously exudes a strong sexuality
- Dislikes the outdoors
- Is in some way an extremist
- Sympathizes with the underdog and envies the succesful without much thought of who deserves what
- Has little interest in other people's resources unless he or she can benefit from them
- Dissipates a great deal of energy trying to alter circumstances beyond his or her control
- Resents needing others
- Has an unstable financial situation
- Feels entitled to criticize others
- Will give a great deal but usually attach strings to their gifts

Gemini North Node
You need to share your awareness with others.

Sagittarius South Node
Yeah, but I don't want to stick around explaining things. I can't learn anything that way.

Problems
An obsession with learning but no interest in using your knowledge in any practical way. Difficulty establishing lasting relationships leads to over-valuation of books, classes and other intellectual activities that provide indirect communication.

Possible reasons

A need for long-term concentration on study or some sort of cultural, ethnic or religious difference has interfered with the formation of relationships. A speech impediment has caused you to turn to books instead of people. A literary career limits people contact. Dependency on reading as an escape from a boring routine. Poor judgement about people has caused you to place your trust only in "proven" sources of information. A lack of concentration has led to communication problems and misunderstandings. A need to conquer an ingrained feeling of stupidity or inferiority.

Possible solutions

Develop your latent communication skills. Channel your intellect instead of being a slave to it. Share your knowledge with others so they can learn. Become a professional trivia expert, con artist, or perpetual student.

Observation

Gemini north node can be a good talker, but he or she is often a poor communicator. He or she is good at tossing out facts, lecturing, impressing others with long streams of beautiful words or technical jargon and so on. But he or she quite often talks at others rather than to them. The Gemini north node tends to quote books verbatim, drop names, quibble over semantics. He or she talks skillfully about facts and theories but generally is at a loss when it comes to applying them or sharing his or her feelings about them. In fact, this person generally avoids sharing any facet of his or her personality beyond the intellectual side. This is a shame since north node in Gemini invariably holds great potential for perception. Development of this potential brings a deepening of the intellect so that ideas can be used for the practical betterment of his or her day-to-day relationships and living conditions.

Signs of an over-developed Sagittarius south node are:
- A tendency to flirt, flatter and charm but reveal nothing
- An expectation that others will hinder his or her freedom
- A tendency to ridicule others
- Generally on his or her way somewhere—"only has a minute"

- First instinct is to take off when pressured
- A tendency to promise more than he or she can deliver
- A distrust of security and routine
- Others accuse him or her of being unreliable; he or she feels that it's others who are unreliable
- Enormous faith in the published word
- Uncomfortable with peers in general

Cancer North Node
You need to develop your domestic and nurturing abilities.

Capricorn South Node
Yeah, but I can't take time out from my career.

Problem
You tend to try to fulfill your need for public acclaim without relating it to your inner needs.

Possible reasons
You have developed your logic at the expense of your emotions. You lacked sympathy, nurturing or material security as a child or had these things taken away from you at a crucial time in your life. An ingrained philosophy of "look out for yourself first" has encouraged a misguided sort of selfishness. Lack of recognition as a child has led to an "I'll show them" attitude. An overpowering need to dominate at all costs.

Possible solutions
Learn to view your emotional needs as keys to increased self-esteem. Learn to adapt your wants to your needs. Have a nervous breakdown. Develop an ulcer. Blame your parents for your hang-ups.

Observation
Cancer north node seems to often coincide with institutionalization in childhood. Sometimes this means an orphanage or hospital has played a major role in the development. Other times it indicates a long stint in a boarding school. Sometimes there's a very regimented home life for one reason or another. Or the parents have been cold and strict. Occasionally the Cancer north noder has had uncaring or unfit

parents and consequently became a ward of the court. But more often the parents were merely more concerned with the Cancer north noder as a status symbol than as an emotional being. Usually the parents were very judgmental and placed a heavy emphasis on doing the right thing in terms of living up to other people's expectations. Thus the Cancer north noder is conditioned to view the game of life materially. But regardless of his or her successes or failures, he or she often feels a great sense of something missing until the Cancer potential for emotional self-preservation and caring is tapped.

Signs of an over-developed Capricorn south node are:
- Dislike of domesticity
- A stubbornly narrow outlook
- Self-consciousness
- Prudishness
- Unapproachability
- Tendency to constantly test others in some way
- Nervousness
- Dislike of new or different ideas
- A desire for respect and honor at any cost
- A tendency to curry favors or social-climb

Leo North Node
You need to learn to love deeply.

Aquarius South Node
Who me? Whaddaya mean? I love absolutely everybody. Except for my ex-best-friend and my ex-lover, and that snooty sales clerk who implied I had no taste....

Problems
You're looking for utopia. Your ideals have frustrated your needs for love and companionship.

Possible reason
You're inclined to be lazy about developing your creativity, preferring to idealize others' accomplishments at the expense of your own. You spend most of your time serving others' causes at the expense of fulfilling your own goals. Traumatic experiences have caused you to retreat from the world to some extent. Ingrained snobbishness hinders the formation of relationships. A subconscious superiority complex.

Possible solutions

Get in touch with your need for dignity and channel it properly. Discover and use your fertile imagination. Learn to lie skillfully. Have a lot of lovers. Devote yourself totally to a humanitarian organization, cause, or activity.

Observations

North node in Leo almost always has some degree of untapped creativity. Sometimes shyness keeps it untapped. The shyness is in itself a manifestation of the untapped Leo north node potentials, since Leo is the sign of confidence. South node in Aquarius encourages the individual to lose himself or herself in a whirl of friendships and acquaintance-making or in some vast utopian ideal. In either case, the motivation is to avoid having to come to terms with his or her own individuality. These people are seldom recognized as shy because their shyness manifests on a personal rather than a public level.

Another manifestation of Leo north node–Aquarius south node imbalance is seen in the person who leaves more prosaic creativities untapped while he or she searches for that great talent that will make a contribution to the world. The Leo north noder isn't content to enjoy developing his or her creativity unless he or she can make a great artistic, dramatic or social contribution to posterity.

In my experience, people with an over-developed Aquarius south node are generally:

- Kept busy dealing with other people's problems
- Wanting to be in the spotlight but often find their contributions get obscured
- Egotistical in an unusual way. They emphasize equality and refuse to acknowledge that some people have more potential than others. In other words, you can't do any more than they can
- Intellectual at the expense of their emotions
- Spiteful
- Fond of shocking others
- Extremist in their work for change
- Contradictory. The brain doesn't know what the heart wants
- Averse to traditional marriage. Women are often

militantly liberated to the point where they resent or dislike men in general
- Believe everything you tell them about themselves as long as it's flattering.

Virgo North Node
You need to learn to work.

Pisces South Node
Yeah, but that means giving up my privacy.

Problem
Inability to analyze feelings.

Possible reasons
Excessive tolerance of unacceptable behavior from others. Faulty reasoning. A tendency to gloss over flaws. A tendency to help others while letting your own life disintegrate. Escapist tendencies. Early upbringing has led to a "you owe me" attitude. Your senses are over-active, overwhelming your logic.

Possible solutions
Channel your fantasies into creative work—poetry, fiction, psychology, etc. Learn to rule your senses instead of letting them rule you. Learn to lie skillfully. Shun human contact as much as possible. Over-eat, drink too much, get stoned.

Observation
Health problems are a frequent manifestation of the Virgo north node—Pisces south node imbalance. These may be physical or mental, real or imagined. Both fear of people and excessive dependency are common—sometimes simultaneously. Compulsive over-eating or an obsession with thinness can be a manifestation. Occasionally I've seen this position in what I call the spiritual or psychological hypochondriac who drifts from guru to soothsayer to therapist looking for someone capable of solving his or her problems for him or her. Invariably, there's a craving for happiness; however, the client can't generally define what this happiness would entail, except to say there would be "no more problems". Well-being improves when the Virgo north node's potential for objectivity and practicality is channeled into some sort of meaningful work.

Some signs of an over-developed Pisces south node are:
- Excessive daydreaming
- Constant requests for help
- A "too sweet for words" facade
- Strange attitudes towards work
- Little control over emotions
- Masochistic or morbid tendencies
- Overall discontentment with his or her lot in life
- Shallowness or game-playing
- Moodiness
- A tendency to attract chaotic conditions and disorganized people.

You might think that the other six nodal positions would be exactly opposite to those described. While they can be, there are often variations on the themes already presented, as you will see.

Libra North Node

You need to learn to cooperate and get along better with others.

Aries South Node

Yeah, but they never want to go along with my plans.

Problems

You have an exaggerated need to prove yourself. You tend to be uncomfortable in social situations. Because of your upbringing you've come to place too high a value on assertiveness.

Possible solutions

Stabilize your relationships in terms of give and take. Learn to differentiate between caring and controlling. Learn to let others have a chance to decide for themselves. Stifle your need for others and look out for yourself.

Observations

South node in Aries often complains of having been forced into something which has irrevocably fouled up his or her life. This could be a too-early marriage, a career, a specific mode of behavior, etc. In any case, he or she, as a result of this experience, justifies his or her reluctance to cooperate in other areas. Aries south node generally hasn't developed his or her ability to commit himself or herself in a long-term situation. He or she wants fast results. If these aren't forthcoming, cooperation is curtailed. Aries south node is also generally unwilling to take responsibility for the effects of his or her actions on other people. He or she is sometimes unwilling to share. The Aries south noder generally wants exclusive rights to what he or she is interested in. He or she feels that future well-being depends on immediate gratification and success. However, goals can often be attained only when the Libra north node's ability to cooperate is tapped and developed.

Signs of an over-balanced Aries south node are:
• High blood pressure
• Impulsiveness
• Hyperactivity
• A cold, critical attitude towards others' accomplishments
• Argumentativeness
• A tendency to brag about accomplishments and be a poor loser
• An insistence on leading
• An uncooperative attitude
• Difficulty in finishing what he or she has started
• Boredom or a short attention span.

Scorpio North Node
You must learn to accept (or give) financial and other types of help when necessary.

Taurus South Node
Yeah, but if you can't earn it (or do it) yourself, you don't deserve it.

Problem
A hang-up about power.

Possible reasons
A repressive environment has made you feel that it's you against the world. A lack of understanding of your environment. A refusal to help unless there's something in it for you. An upbringing where there's been an over-emphasis on money, things, or importance.

Possible solutions

Become more active in joint endeavours—a business partnership, encounter group, community project, etc. Sharpen and develop your imagination. Concentrate on material growth regardless of what happens. Give all your money and possessions to a guru or religious sect and let them provide for you.

Observation

Taurus south node often tries to make willpower a substitute for insight. He or she feels that by developing his or her willpower he or she will be able to handle whatever curves life throws them. He or she is often especially fond of simplistic self-help books and success formulas that promise unlimited earnings. Now there's nothing wrong with wanting to help yourself. And no one would deny the importance of willpower. We've already seen what problems can arise when you don't build up your own resources. But all the money, power and determination in the world is useless unless you know where your problems are coming from. Developing the Scorpio north node's potential for insight will improve success potential drastically.

Signs of an over-developed Taurus south node are:
- Refusal to think about anything that's not backed up by conclusive and irrevocable proof
- Insensitivity; disregard for other's rights
- Shyness
- Everything viewed in terms of money
- Excessive introversion
- Shrewdness rather than intelligence
- Self-indulgence
- Very conservative or "dated" manner of dress or speech
- Vanity but no real confidence
- Cowardice.

Sagittarius North Node

You should follow through on your interest in psychology, travel, etc.

Gemini South Node

Yeah, but my day-to-day activities don't leave me any time. Besides, I hate studying.

Problem

A mental block prevents expansion.

Possible reasons

Environmental restrictions hindered learning. Refusal to take chances. Dislike of reading or distrust of any type of indirect communication. Reluctance to be put in a position where you may be asked to give advice, teach, etc. An upbringing that encouraged superficiality. Little success with early education.

Possible solutions

Take interest courses. Loosen stifling ties and routines. Sever all ties and spend your time drifting.

Observation

You'll remember that we said Gemini north node relies on book learning to replace awareness. With Gemini south node, the tables are turned. Knowledge remains at a very rudimentary level. There can be an "I read it in the Enquirer so it must be true" philosophy. Or there can be a distrust of any information that comes from afar. In other words, the local news commentator knows what he's talking about but the foreign news commentator's full of bull unless he's voicing the same opinion. Frequently, Gemini south node relies on rumors, gossip and small talk to form the basis of his or her knowledge. College education is looked on with suspicion; in fact, sometimes there's a reverse snobbism in connection with education. Gemini south node tends to be content with his or her knowledge no matter how incomplete it is. It's only when the Gemini south node is suddenly thrust into a new environment or routine that he or she becomes aware that something's missing. At that point, he or she can tap the Sagittarius north node's potential and expand his or her knowledge and understanding of the world.

The person with an over-developed Gemini south node:
• Has few long-range goals
• Is restricted by his or her routine or environment

- Is immature or retains an emphsis on dressing and acting like he or she did at a much younger age
- Sees no point in college unless it's a prerequisite to a certain job
- Does not like to waste time on abstractions or unproven theories
- May be fickle
- May be a bigot
- Is sarcastic or cynical
- Marries a childhood sweetheart, neighbor, high school friend, etc.
- Usually marries early and settles into a routine where the only big change is a transition from school to work
- Loves travel as long as the place visited isn't too different from what he or she is used to.

Capricorn North Node
You should take steps towards a career (or honors or increased self-esteem).

Cancer South Node
Yeah, but what would my kids (or parents or boss) do without me?

Problem
You've adopted real or imagined responsibilities to others that are keeping you from becoming all that you can become.

Possible reasons
Fear of public exposure. Lack of planning. A feeling that you're unworthy in some way. Refusal to let others lead their own lives.

Possible solutions
Take cautious steps towards the careers, honors, or recognition you want. Examine your needs and responsibilities honestly and take necessary steps to balance them. Get a divorce. Commit suicide. Study the lives and actions of others who have done what you want to do and pattern your life after theirs if at all possible.

Observation

Cancer south node tends towards deeply-rooted compulsive behavior patterns which allow him or her to justify failures. Justification of this sort is a form of dishonesty. This prevents the development of Capricorn north node's considerable untapped potential for self-esteem. It also prevents the formation of deep relationships since if you're not honest with yourself you can't possibly be honest with others. Cancer south node easily becomes bogged down in dependency on those who need him or her until personal discontent forces development of Capricorn's north node potential.

Some typical manifestations of an over-developed Cancer south node are:
- An overall lack of success in life
- Hypersensitivity and sloppy sentimentality
- Fear of authority figures
- Childishness
- Lack of emotional self-control
- Lack of self-confidence
- Snobbishness alternating with blind acceptance of others
- Self-pity
- Excessive complaining
- A craving for emotional attention.

Aquarius North Node
Your lovers should also be friends.

Leo South Node
Yeah, but that's not romantic.

Problem
Lack of detachment.

Possible reasons

An excessive craving for warmth. A tendency to close your eyes to unpleasant truths. Misuse of power potential. A tendency to attach strings to any help you give. Self-concern blinds you to other people's needs. Or maybe you use romantic courtship rituals as a means of postponing having to display the real you.

Possible solutions

Give of yourself without demanding anything in return. Channel your imagination into beneficial group activities, reform work, etc. Display the courage of your convictions. Worry excessively about the impression you make.

Observation

Leo south node craves involvement—in fun, in creative projects, in love, whatever. But without developing the Aquarius north node's potential for detachment, the end result is quantity without quality. Leo south node finds it virtually impossible to come into contact with another person without getting involved. Since these involvements tend to be made in the heat of the moment, however, they often prove unfulfilling in the long-run. The solution is to develop the Aquarius north node's detachment, rationality and independence.

Some typical indications of an over-balanced Leo south node are:

- Exaggeration
- A need to be the center of attention
- Many acquaintances, few real friends
- A tendency to show off his or her body or wardrobe
- A "what will people think" approach to things
- Dependency on others to reinforce confidence
- Smugness
- A belief that some people are just plain inferior, no matter what they do
- Much artsy-fartsy dabbling
- A theatrical or melodramatic type of self-projection.

Pisces North Node

You must learn to sacrifice, give in, or give up.

Virgo South Node

Yeah, but I have too much invested.

Problem

Lack of understanding of need priorities.

Possible reasons

Excessive stubbornness. Fear of being taken advantage of. Self-destructive tendencies. Refusal to face the fact that some problems are difficult to solve totally. An excessively critical environment makes it hard to admit defeat. Guilt over past wrong-doing or failures.

Possible solutions

Learn to relax. Temper your analytic tendencies with compassion for yourself and others. Judge people and things by their usefullness and set your priorities accordingly.

Observation

Virgo south node often doesn't enjoy his or her own company. This naturally affects his or her ability to enjoy relationships, since the self is always present. Virgo south node doesn't feel human; he or she operates like a well-run machine. Not all Virgo south nodes are workaholics, but I've seen enough instances to believe that this is one of the more typical results of nodal imbalance for this polarity. Another is an involvement in unsatisfying or destructive relationships, since often the Virgo south noder is so terrified of being alone that any relationship is better than no relationship. By tapping the hidden strength of Pisces north node, the individual can get in touch with his or her basic humanness. Only then can he or she come to terms with his or her needs and alleviate his or her dissatisfaction.

Some signs of an over-developed south node in Virgo are:
• Bigotry
• Refusal to settle for anything less than perfect
• A feeling of being "different"
• A tendency to test others mentally
• A "let me do it for you" approach
• Shyness
• Jealousy
• Tendency to be critical of other's grooming, clothing or abilities in general
• Pettiness
• Insecurity; builds himself or herself up by knocking others down openly or through back-stabbing.

Again, I stress that these are typical manifestations and urge you to look for variations on these themes.

Some of you may feel that I'm being harsh or overly judgmental. You must remember here that we're talking about a negative potential, an undesirable lack of development of particular qualities, stumbling-blocks that are keeping us from growing. It would be nice to say that these are actually blessings in disguise, but that's over-simplifying the thing. Problems remain problems until you confront them and do something about them. Hence all this talk on balancing the nodal polarities.

A few words should be said about the interpretations in general. Most of the clients and students I've presented this material to have acknowledged problems similar to those mentioned and feel they have at least two or three of the symptoms of unbalanced nodes. In general, these are people who are very self-aware and are interested in making the most of their potential. So if in reading your nodal interpretation you found some symptoms or problem areas, don't panic. Chances are you're trying to balance your nodes or you wouldn't be aware of your problems.

A few students also mentioned that although they didn't find the nodal interpretations too valid for their own positions, they felt a strong affinity to the opposite positions. Some felt both the true positions and the reversed positions had some validity. These are also people who are trying to balance their nodes, but they're in general presently overcompensating for the south node. In other words, having discovered the north node potential, they're concentrating on it alone without taking into account that the south node potential, if used in moderation, can be a beneficial and balancing influence. They're at a stage where they're totally denying the well-developed south node, even though it has proved useful in the past and certainly should not be dismissed as a total liability.

A small minority found no validity in either interpretation. Some of these people responded more strongly to the nodes by house position, but others saw no validity in these either. These people were in general more discontented, less open, and more inclined to want reassurance that the future held a marriage, raise, or some other bit of good luck. In general, these people seemed to lack self-awareness, to deny their strengths and be more certain that their problems stemmed from bad breaks or something someone did to them rather than from any failing on their parts. They described themselves generally in terms like "I'll do anything for a friend", "I'm too loyal for my own good"; "I'm always optimistic"; "I'm a sucker for a sob story"—all passively negative qualities stemming from exploiting a virtue and carrying it to excess. These were the people who seemed to be most typical of the unbalanced node Yeah-But syndrome.

Now I don't mean to say that if you disagree totally with my interpretations that your nodes are unbalanced, but I would say that you should get an honest, objective friend who knows you to comment on the sections that apply to you. Remember, the retrograde condition of the nodes can sometimes make tendencies express subconsciously. On the other hand, you may become one of those rare people who has managed to balance your nodes. If so, you're to be congratulated!

In summary, the north node's sign always shows what you must do to find the "something missing" in your life. The south node always offers some excuse for not doing what you need to do. The excuses can seem very reasonable if taken at face value. However, if the excuse is examined closely, you will invariably see that it masks some sort of fear that must be overcome.

The problem represented, or a similar one, is the reason for your discontent. Balance the nodes and the problem will resolve itself.

It's presently fashionable to believe that we choose to have problems, either to pay off some karmic debt, to make us more perfect, or to fulfill some subconscious or karmic need. Without getting involved in the pros and cons of the theory of reincarnation, I think it's safe to say that no one who lives on this earth is perfect. We all have some feelings of inadequacy, either based on fact, on past experiences, or on an ignorance of our own potentials.

Problems develop for a variety of reasons. Primarily they develop from faulty interaction with others. This faulty interaction generally stems from two sources—lack of self-knowledge and lack of understanding of other people. Now few people purposely choose to remain ignorant. Fear of knowledge is conditioned, sometimes purposely, other times unconsciously. Quite often this conditioning begins in childhood when you lack the maturity to undertand the true nature of events around you.

Let's take an example: A young couple marry. The bride is nine weeks pregnant. The baby is born on schedule, weighing seven pounds plus. Now this is a small town, so naturally there's a certain amount of discussion about the baby's lack of prematurity, especially since the mother is the daughter of a prominent local minister.

The mother is happy with both her marriage and motherhood in general. But having been brought up to believe that premarital sex is a sin, she also feels a certain amount of guilt. This makes her extremely defensive—especially where her child is concerned. She's determined to make certain that no one will be able to say that she's not a good mother and does what she can to insure that the child knows nothing of its conception out of wedlock.

As the child grows up, it is overprotected and pampered. Mother discourages the child from making friends with anyone who might know that she was "born early". Mother chalks up the child's feuds with peers to parental prejudices. When the child asks normal questions about "when did you and Daddy meet, marry, etc.", Mother grows noticeably tense and quickly changes the subject.

The child grows up feeling that there's some tragic flaw in her character. Unable to find out what it is, she withdraws more and more from people until she eventually finds it impossible to relate to anyone. At this point, psychiatric help becomes necessary.

Obviously, the initial problem was the mother's. But because the mother governed the child's environment for many years, her problem became her daughter's problem too. The daughter was unaware of the real nature of the problem. All she knew was that by her mother's actions it was obvious that she saw her daughter as weak and strange. Since these were mother's expectations—expressed subconsciously—the daughter, who in childhood had little choice but to follow her mother's wishes, lived up to her expectations.

Sounds like a far-fetched rationale for having a nervous breakdown, doesn't it? But many cases of maladjustment are based on incidents that in themselves seem far more trivial. The key is that these incidents happen before we can understand why they're happening and where they're coming from. Because they can't be dealt with openly and rationally, they go inward and become nagging worries which the imagination blows out of all proportion.

According to astrology, the birth chart shows not only the problems but the potential solutions as well. I've mentioned some of these earlier in the chapter and will be discussing them at great length in another chapter. Now, no doubt some of you will disagree with some of these. You'll say that a hasty marriage, a nervous breakdown, a disregard for your conscience, etc. is not a good solution. And probably you're right. But the fact remains that they are solutions. Many people choose them—like our young girl above whose nervous breakdown justified her feelings of strangeness.

The point we must keep in mind is that there are solutions that will lead to growth and help develop the "something missing" and there are cop-out solutions that will lead to stagnation. Using astrology to understand the significance of the nodal sign polarities is a crucial step in learning to choose our solutions wisely.

House Positions:
Conflict of Interest

We've already learned that the sign positions of the nodes show us our path to growth and our reasons for choosing not to grow. Now we must expand on this information by seeing what areas of our lives are most affected by our choices. To do this, we must look at the nodal house positions.

As you know, each house represents a specific area of your life. Any planet or sensitive point in a house will emphasize that house's function in your life.

You also should know that each pair of houses has a certain relationship of function. Let's run through these briefly:

First:	True self-projection	*Seventh:*	Self-projection modified to attract others
Second:	Earning for self	*Eighth:*	Earnings shared with others
Third:	Education for survival	*Ninth:*	Education for understanding
Fourth:	Private life	*Tenth:*	Public life
Fifth:	Personal pleasures	*Eleventh:*	Shared pleasures
Sixth:	Physical well-being	*Twelfth:*	Spiritual well-being

Often it happens that one house of a pair will be occupied while the other remains empty. In this case, the one function predominates over the other. For example, let's say a person has Venus in the sixth house while the twelfth remains untenanted. This person will invariably be more concerned with physical well-being than spiritual well-being, although interest in the one doesn't necessarily preclude interest in the other.

If, in the case described, the twelfth house was also occupied by say, Saturn, with Saturn opposing Venus, the situation would be slightly different. Now, both sixth and twelfth demand attention and Venus and Saturn may set up a feud about what's going to get priority. When this happens, one of three outcomes is possible: the planets can continue to feud so that neither priority gets adequate attention; one priority can be sacrificed for the sake of the other; or the planets can compromise and spend half their time cooperating on each priority.

Since the nodes are always in opposition, there's always an element of conflict of interests. On the surface, the solution looks deceptively simple—since it's easier to rely on the south node and do what comes naturally, it would be easy to sacrifice the north node's potential. But, as we've already seen, that potential must be integrated; otherwise, we feel inner discontent that may eventually affect our outer lives.

Following are some typical conflicts of interest, some typical results of sacrificing the north node, and some possible ways of effecting a workable compromise:

First House North Node vs. Seventh House South Node Conflicts

Good self-projection in terms of being true to self vs. good self-projection in terms of appealing to others.

Excessive worry about partner's well-being vs. attention to your own well-being.

Self-generated vitality vs. dependence on others for stimulating vitality.

Possible Results of Sacrificing North Node

You become dependent on the cooperation of others. You lose awareness of your own feelings about things. You lose your identity. You sacrifice yourself so that others can achieve their goals.

Possible Ways to Integrate North Node

Learn to accept leadership roles occassionally. Remain sensitive to your environment but try to avoid being overly influenced by it. Travel—preferably on your own. Seek direct, honest contact with others. Seek out new experiences.

Second House North Node vs. Eighth House South Node Conflicts

Personal worth vs. worth to others.

Practicality vs. sensuality.

Ability to influence others vs. ability to be influenced by others.

Possible Results of Sacrificing North Node

Extravagance. Involvement in shady dealings. Creation of false values. Lack of discrimination. Misuse of sex, occult knowledge or joint resources.

Possible ways to Integrate North Node

Earn what you accept. Seek possessions for their practicality or intrinsic beauty rather than for their value as status symbols. Keep some strength in reserve for your own needs rather than using it all in pleasing others. Invest in known commodities rather than high-risk ventures. Keep spending slightly behind income.

Third House North Node vs. Ninth House South Node Conflicts

Good practical education vs. mind expansion. Familiar day-to-day contacts (siblings, neighbors, school chums) vs. new contacts (in-laws, foreigners, people whose experiences are different from yours). Liking for your environment vs. desire to explore new areas.

Possible Results of Sacrificing North Node

Lack of concern with education's practical application. Extensive contacts lead to loss of touch with family, old friends etc. Adoption of a guru facade. Craving for travel causes drifting. Superficial intellectualism replaces true understanding.

Possible Ways to Integrate North Node

Travel, with an eye to successfully settling down somewhere. Strive to understand, and make yourself understood to siblings, close kin, etc. Study with an eye to using your knowledge. Share your practical knowledge. Use your common sense.

Fourth House North Node vs. Tenth House South Node
Conflicts

Pleasant home life vs. pleasant career. Worries about career vs. attention to private life. Private doubts vs. public self-esteem.

Possible Results of Sacrificing North Node

Loss of dignity. Tendency to insist on getting recognition as boss. Tendency to take on a big daddy facade (no, this isn't strictly a male trait, even if it's thought of as a male stereotype).

Possible Ways to Integrate North Node

Develop maturity. Use your untapped potential to strengthen your foundations. Examine your roots, upbringing and prejudices for keys to the reasons for your self-doubts. Take notice of your domestic needs.

Fifth House North Node vs. Eleventh House South Node
Conflicts

Pleasurable childrearing vs. pleasurable social life. Romance vs. friendship. Creative ambitions vs. social or humanitarian ambitions.

Possible Results of Sacrificing North Node

Impracticality. Tendency to think instead of act. Mental drifting and daydreaming. Undervaluation of creativity or procreation. Frustrated hopes.

Possible Ways to Integrate North Node

Fulfill dreams in a practical way. Develop potential for enjoying leisure time in an active, tangible way. Exploit ability to bring pleasure to others. Examine feelings about children, childrearing and procreation. Don't use group priorities as an excuse for neglecting your personal goals.

Sixth House North Node vs. Twelfth House South Node
Conflicts

Physical health vs. spiritual health. Efficiency vs. debilitating worries. Pride in work vs. feelings of inferiority.

Possible Results of Sacrificing North Node

Reclusive tendencies. Feelings of alienation. Escapism, paranoia. Lack of detachment.

Possible Ways to Integrate North Node

Learn to take pleasure in helping others. Organize and discipline your mind. Accept appreciation. Be willing to work for others. Develop practical goals.

Seventh House North Node vs. First House South Node Conflicts

Marriage vs. independence. Accepting vs. demanding. Overcoming enmity vs. comfortable self-projection.

Possible Results of Sacrificing North Node

Excessive worry about being beaten or outdone. Inability to relate to others. Feelings of martyrdom, excessive egotism, loneliness. A tendency to interfere with other's free-will. Belittling other's worth.

Possible Ways to Integrate North Node

Whole-hearted giving. Increase your consideration of others. Take an objective look at how others respond to your self-projection and do what you can to improve it. Detach yourself from your overconcern with your image. Channel your energies into marriage and other one-to-one relationships.

Eighth House North Node vs. Second House South Node Conflicts

Own values vs. other's values. Growth vs. degeneration. Joint resources vs. personal resources.

Possible results of Sacrificing North Node

Extreme possessiveness. Sexual difficulties. Lack of regard for other people's values or needs. Unhappiness with possessions and money, no matter how comfortable your material situation seems to others. In extreme cases, trouble with the law; more often simply trouble from atypical values.

Possible Ways to Integrate the North Node

Develop self-control and self-discipline. Develop an appreciation for life. De-emphasize things; concentrate more on relationships. Organize your life—clear away worthless people, things, attitudes. Try to stop worrying about being appreciated; be willing to work for the joy of working rather than for prestige.

Ninth House North Node vs. Third House South Node Conflicts
Devotion to causes vs. the need for stable routine. Dreams vs. realities. Psychic or intuitive mind vs. logical mind.

Possible Results of Sacrificing North Node
Entanglement in mazes of busy-work, gossip, family feuds, etc. Problems with teachers, in-laws, foreigners. A tendency to take everything too literally; inhibition of the higher mind. Cynicism, agnosticism. Insatiable curiosity bordering on meddling.

Possible Ways to Integrate the North Node
Expand your mind by taking courses. Read about controversial issues and try to formulate opinions. Travel. Be selective about people; avoid gossips and crisis-prone erratic types. Take time out from routine activities to try new things.

Tenth House North Node vs. Fourth House South Node Conflicts
Authority vs. need for private life. Conscious vs. subconscious. Ambitions for power vs. ambitions for self-understanding.

Possible Results of Sacrificing North Node
Family demands are used as an excuse for not developing your fullest potentials. Neglect of career. Parenting or domesticity takes up most of your time. Others take you for granted.

Possible Ways to Integrate the North Node
Untangle yourself from domestic and parental traps. Involve yourself in your community instead of staying home all the time. Develop a more positive outlook. Make contact with people outside your family milieu. Go out to work, even if it's only part-time or volunteer work.

Eleventh House North Node vs. Fifth House South Node Conflicts

Need for social attention vs. need for creative development. Reliability in friendships vs. demands of lovers and children. Fulfillment of dreams vs. fulfillment of present needs.

Possible Results of Sacrificing North Node

Inappropriate behavior in terms of your goals. Difficult love affairs. Desperate measures taken in order to gain recognition. Generosity verging on extravagance. Lack of fulfillment in romance, parenting, social life.

Possible Ways to Integrate North Node

Become goal oriented instead of pleasure oriented. Let love affairs be guided by your self-respect. Temper your generosity with discrimination. Openly admit your weaknesses. Meditate on the value of friendship.

Twelfth House North Node vs. Sixth House South Node Conflicts

Lack of confidence vs. capability. Self-destructive behavior vs. service to others. Reclusive tendencies vs. need to work or serve.

Possible Results of Sacrificing North Node

Crises involving awareness. Physical or mental exhaustion. Inability to find suitable work. Disorganization. Excessive self-criticism that encourages feelings of inferiority.

Possible Ways to Integrate the North Node

Eradicate self-pity. Recognize that an inferiority complex is often a warped superiority complex. Examine your motives for working and serving. Learn to externalize your anger in an appropriate way.

The nodal polarity must be balanced; it does very little good to sacrifice one nodal position for the other. Yet this is the most common tendency when trying to resolve the conflict. The north node isn't always the one sacrificed either, as those who are in the process of balancing their nodes quite often go through an overcompensating phase where the south node is for a time totally denied conscious expression. Thus, the person with north node in the sixth may sometimes experience conditions that are more typical of south node in the sixth.

The house position of the north node invariably points to some hang-up in that area of your life. This hang-up is the underlying source of the conflict.

In the first house, there's a hang-up about leadership. This person is inherently strong and probably highly motivated but often lacks moderation in his or her attempts to fulfill a leadership role. There's a fluctuation between playing the dictator—which invariably proves unsuccessful—and a strong lack of confidence in your abilities. You feel if you can't be the ultimate leader you may as well just put your life in other people's hands. Either extreme produces clashes with others, since neither the dictator nor the pawn proves to be a totally comfortable role.

A less common tendency is to not care about how you look. This person, rightly or wrongly, wants to be accepted on the basis of his or her inner qualities. However, again rightly or wrongly, in our society relationships are often initiated on the basis of an attractive appearance. For this reason, those who neglect to develop this facet of their personality quite often don't get to first base when it comes to forming relationships.

It's interesting to note that in the process of balancing the first/seventh nodal axis, the person may for a time develop an almost narcissistic preoccupation with grooming and appearance.

When the north node is in the second house, there's a hang-up about security. According to what stage of the balancing act the person is in, he or she can exhibit wild extravagance or greed and parsimony. In either case, there's an emphasis on possessions as status symbols. The actual possessions may take various forms—from ultra-expensive to the recycled bargain. In any case, they're only a symptom of the cause, which in reality is a perverted or underdeveloped spirit of enterprise. Sometimes possessions are used to assuage feelings of inadequacy caused by a constitutional weakness, other times they're a means of providing some measure of present security to compensate for a childhood lack. There's a strong tendency to trust to luck or be attracted to get-rich-quick schemes. Often, possessions are gained only to be lost again through extravagance or blind generosity. Sometimes there's a tendency to gamble, with disgrace or disaster ensuing.

When the node takes an avaricious form of expression, chances are that some important form of security was withheld in childhood. Clients with this placing invariably complain of some traumatic lack of privacy. Having to share a room with several siblings, having to conform to stifling regulations while in boarding school, a parent who listened in on phone conversations, opened mail, read diaries, etc.—these are some of the most common experiences mentioned. As a result, these people have come to feel that they have nothing to truly call their own. Thus, even if they should acquire great wealth, they're afraid to give even a little for fear that others will demand more and more until once again everything they have is gone.

This last form of expression may also result from a surfeit of negative eighth house south node experiences in the adult years.

In the third house, there's a hang-up about relationships. This generally stems from repressed or misdirected concentration on one area to the detriment of the other. Problems can range from fanaticism to cynicism. There's often a sense of not belonging which may lead to anything from unhealthy rivalries to bigotry to involvement in cults to extreme misanthropism. In extreme cases, there can be a turning against your own culture and absorption into a completely alien one.

In the fourth house, there's a hang-up about developing or growing up when the north node is present. This can take the form of excessive self-consciousness or it can trigger a lust for power, depending on which node is allowed to dominate. In either case, the feelings of inferiority are based on illogical feelings. These are often a result of childhood experiences. Sometimes death of a parent plays a role. Other times the parent's immaturity or lack of common sense or stability has had a negative impact.

Those people who try to fulfill their excess needs for power often complain of lack of recognition and/or sympathy from those who are in a position to offer advancement.

In the fifth house, there's a hang-up about self-expression. Here we can have the social climber or the show-off. Less commonly we see the "Aw shucks, it was nothing" syndrome. Humility is either lacking or perverted in some way. In some way, the ability to verbalize your attitudes is detrimental to relationship formation. Romance is usually the most common area of difficulty, although parent-child relationships and social life in general can suffer as well. Sometimes there's a tendency to expect your children to do what you couldn't, whether it's marry a millionaire, become a brain surgeon or simply be the most popular child in the class.

In the sixth house there can be hang-ups about imperfections, dedication, or service. Narrow-mindedness and intolerance are frequently at the root of these hang-ups. A lack of confidence and a strong fear of rejection are common side effects. Everything must be black or white; gray is intolerable; "almost" doesn't count at all. This holds true both in self-judgment and in judgment of other people.

Total success is this person's ultimate goal, nothing else is acceptable. There's a tendency to frequently test other people's dedication by throwing out obstacles or challenges which must be met if the tested person wants to retain the esteem and respect of the testee (note that the tester may also be the testee). Extreme urgency is a keynote—there's always some crisis to be solved or some need that must be filled immediately. Otherwise, dissatisfaciton sets in.

Sometimes, the person may retreat from the real world entirely either via the nervous breakdown route or through involvement in some idealistic pursuit.

Typically, this person makes excessive demands on himself or herself and talks a great deal about "good" and "bad" people, things, and attitudes. He or she is generally disappointed in friends, work and everything else because expectations are set at such an unreasonably high level.

In the seventh house, there can be hang-ups about harmony or cooperation. Depending on the phase of nodal balance, the person can be far too easily influenced or far too convinced that his or her way is the only way. The underlying cause of this is a lack of firm partnership goals. This person is torn between involvement at any cost and preservation of his or her highly comfortable image of self as a good or beautiful person.

Less frequently, there's an inability for the small talk and role playing that's necessary to attract others. This seems to be a problem connected to the overcompensation phase of nodal balance.

With the north node in the eighth house, the hang-up seems to be centered around power. Inability to forgive and grudge-holding are common expressions of this hang-up. A muddled or twisted sexual identity is another manifestation. Thus we see the macho male, the femme fatale and the asexual being—as well as those who are attracted to these types. Often there's a "money is power" syndrome that can manifest in gambling or foolish spending. In most cases there's a strong desire to prove your worth or to get back at those who have wronged you.

In the ninth house, the hang-up centers around education or learning and a lack of self-restraint invariably plays a major role. This person is often so easily swayed by his or her environment that life is spent moving from one bandwagon to another. A lack of continuity is often seen, too, making a little learning truly a potentially dangerous thing. Occasionally we find the reverse intellectual snob, one who values manual dexterity in just about any form but has no use for mental dexterity.

In the tenth house, the hang-up is connected with respect or integrity which may mask a basic dislike of people and/or social functions. This person subconsciously fears authority figures and is uncomfortable in society unless he or she can come out decked in all the trappings of success—and even then there may be doubts as to the worth of that success. Reclusiveness or deep introversion may manifest as a means of coping with these fears.

Often there's been an early struggle with authority figures or society in general. Difficulties with one or both parents are common. Usually the early upbringing involves a heavy dose of moralistic philosophy. Less frequently, one or both parents was maladjusted and the offspring has to live down their misdeeds or grows up feeling a need to make amends for his or her parents failure to contribute to society.

In the eleventh house, hang-ups can involve honesty, knowledge, or ethics—all things that would seem to correlate more with Sagittarius/ninth house at first glance. But where north node in Sagittarius/ninth leans towards lack of discrimination and sometimes fanaticism, the eleventh house north node takes a cold, dispassionate approach. Whatever is perceived to be the truth or the right way is followed without thought about damage that may be done should honesty prove not to be the best policy or if the truth turns out to be flawed. Relationships are often spoiled by this "honesty is the only policy" approach as others frequently feel demeaned by this brutal, almost egotistical honesty.

Occasionally north node in the eleventh house can manifest in a compulsive need to see the good side in everyone, regardless of the cost to self. Here we see the Mr. or Ms. Nice who suffers extensive guilt pangs if the need to criticize arises. A child-like Pollyannaism and naivete about people eventually leads to disappointments and being taken advantage of in relationships.

In the twelfth house, the hang-up is connected with self-understanding. The problem often stems from a combination of fatalism and a lack of determination. Because of a lack of appreciation for self, this person craves appreciation from others to foster self-worth. But because self-worth can only be gained from within, external appreciation seldom changes this person's perceptions. Self-sabotaging and illness are manifestations of this confused, inferior concept of self-potential.

Sometimes this nodal position manifests in an inability to share feelings or just plain shyness. Quite often in childhood this person suffered experiences that made him or her withdrawn or unreachable. Sometimes these involve parents, other times they took place in the early school environment. Sulking, brooding and depression are common.

For the astrologer, Yeah-buts, conflicts and hang-ups require extremely delicate handling. Obviously, it wouldn't be wise to tell a client that his or her problems stem from innate hypocrisy, narrow-mindedness or whatever. Yet at the same time, it does no good to couch problem areas in the beautiful but ambiguous phrases popular in some humanistic circles. After all, a problem is a problem and if the client doesn't understand its source, he will have no way of solving it.

Perceptiveness on your part, combined with tactful questioning and a full understanding of why the client has consulted you should give you a sound idea of how to present the problem of nodal imbalance. These are factors that no book can impart. However, if you familiarize yourself with the typical manifestations of nodal imbalance, it should be easier for you to help your client gain understanding.

The Nodes as Symbols of Dreams and Self-perceived Reality

*T*he sign and house positions of the nodes quite often show the dichotomy between the dreamed-of self and the actual self or self-perceived self. This is a very good starting point for the counselling astrologer to begin from in any discussion of nodal imbalance, since the client (unless he or she is of the old school who believes the astrologer knows everything and shouldn't need to ask questions) will be given the chance to talk about what's missing, and the astrologer can then get into a discussion of how to correct the imbalance without getting into a lot of judgmental claptrap that might alienate the client.

However, it's not realistic to expect each and every client to be open or comfortable about discussing their dreams and failings. Some will have trouble expressing themselves. Others may lack the necessary self-awareness or objectivity for this kind of exercise. Still others are enamored of the old-style astrology. This last type is quite often very suspicious of any request for information that can't be given in monosyllables.

For this reason, it may be useful to have some idea of how these dreams manifest and how they stand up against reality.

North node in Aries wants to be outgoing. He or she wants to be a self-starter, well able to lead and assertive enough to get what he or she wants. In contrast, this person is generally well-liked but inclined to see himself or herself as passive or too shy. There's usually an interest in or talent for art, fashion, editing, publicizing, or some other Libra-ruled talent but because the person seldom challenges that talent by doing anything innovative, he or she gets passed by when the acclaim is handed out and may begin to feel resentful. He or she can be sympathetic to the point of becoming a doormat and may become so enmeshed in other's struggles for success and happiness that his or her own needs remain unfulfilled.

North node in Taurus wants money, or at least a reputation as a connoisseur. He or she wants the good things in life. He or she wants to be thought of as firm, patient, and lacking nothing. In contrast, the person is generally someone who's undergone drastic changes of values or circumstance, intense discomfort of some sort, or traumatic experiences. His or her routine is periodically stirred up and shifted as a result of emotional upheavals or disturbances that are seemingly beyond his or her control. He or she tends to be jealous of others who seem to have attained more in life and may develop a rather pessimistic attitude in terms of realizing his or her dreams. He or she may compensate for lack of material security by trying to possess people, or may compensate for emotional losses by developing a reclusive streak. These tendencies only serve to trigger more problems.

North node in Gemini dreams of a life of variety. He or she wants to be seen as adaptable and a good conversationalist. He or she also wants to be thought of as an educated person. In reality, this is a person who transmutes emotions into interests. He or she is interested in spirituality, education, travel, and similar Sagittarius-ruled things, but in a passive, abstract way rather than in terms of experiencing and enriching the life. He or she may mix well with others, but only as long as he or she can assume the role of teacher. This teaching isn't necessarily a formal or professional role, but it permeates most interactions just the same, and in the course of assuming this role, much of north node in Gemini's enthusiasm for life is misused or wasted. Extremism of some sort may also mar conversational skills.

North node in Cancer consciously or subconsciously feels that his or her strong emotions will act as a deterrent to his or her happiness, so a primary dream theme involves keeping emotions under control or else finding someone who will appreciate his or her emotionality so that it will no longer be a threat. He or she wants to be attached to someone else who will offer protection from the cold cruel world and guarantee a measure of emotional security. This person generally represses emotions. He or she is often confused about his or her feelings and finds it difficult to relate to others on an emotional level. Sometimes the tendency to fear emotions comes out as a cynical or pessimistic streak designed to camouflage the person's vulnerability.

North node in Leo would like to be seen as someone with a tremendous amount of vitality. He or she wants to be known as someone who's attained creative or business success. He or she may aspire to be a famous movie star or politician, or may want to be known for his or her lovely home or lavish parties. He or she wants to be respected and able to impress others. This person is social and capable of expressing emotion, albeit in a rather detached way. He or she may have some rather funny loyalties or a misconception of loyalty. This may serve to prevent success, as the person is inclined to be afraid that his success might inconvenience or be unfair to others. This preoccupation with the good of the group, as opposed to his or her own good, can lead to unpredictable behavior that brings more controversy than respect.

North node in Virgo dreams of being the trusted second-in-command without whom things would fall apart. He or she wants to be a policy-maker or manager, or at least the chief executive's right-hand person. He or she wants to be known as someone who can't be deceived or boondoggled. This is generally a quiet person whose feelings are more important than logic in terms of outlining a direction in life. Instead of a policy-maker, he or she is generally a dreamer whose dreams seldom become realities. He or she lacks—or at least hasn't developed—the analytical abilities inherent in the Virgo north node. He or she is vague about goals and vaguer still about how to realize them.

North node in Libra dreams of happiness and harmony. He or she would like to be known as a very sociable person. Others play a very important role in this person's dreams. In contrast, this is an enthusiastic, emotionally active person whose selfishness may interfere with social interaction and harmony in general.

North node in Scorpio consciously or subconsciously wants to be tested. He or she wants to experience the highest and lowest phases of existence in order to get in touch with his or her deepest emotions and learn to balance them. He or she wants a crash course in living and experiencing. In contrast, we find a person with good common sense and rather repressed emotions. He or she clings to home, possessions, and routines in a way that keeps life on an even keel, devoid of major highs or lows. Conservatism often squelches this person's dreams.

North node in Sagittarius wants to be thought of as natural, sincere, intellectual, refined, and broad-minded. This is a person of such changeable emotions that he or she may be mistaken for a yes-person or a phoney. He or she has trouble focusing on one thing at a time, and tends to scatter energy to the point where objectives seldom reach completion. Restlessness keeps dreams in an ever-changing state so that they may never be clearly defined. In effect, this person might dream of having a dream.

North node in Capricorn tends to dream very traditional dreams. He or she wants to be a law-maker, a policy-maker, an organizer, an Einstein, or at least a manager. He or she wants to be known for objectivity, prudence, and good leadership ability. He or she wants to stand out against the backdrop of ordinary workers as someone who know where he or she is going and is getting there. In contrast, this is an emotional, rather touchy person. He or she is fond of comfort and reluctant to make changes. The need for emotional security dominates the need for dream fulfillment to the point where changes in residence, job situation, public notice, or whatever become extremely upsetting, even if these changes herald better things.

North node in Aquarius dreams of freedom, of transcending the limitations of his or her structure environment and being able to do whatever he or she wants without interference. He or she might dream of self-employment or a career in science, teaching, or some other humanitarian field. This person dreams of the day when he or she can be independent of others except on his or her terms. In contrast, this person is inclined to be rather star-struck or at least in awe of authority figures. At the same time, he or she has very definite opinions which are swayed only on the basis of irrevocable evidence that they're wrong. This person is outgoing and inclined to get out and socialize as much as possible. The needs for independence conflict and often sabotage each end of the nodal need scale. Only when the needs are reconciled will fulfillment be found.

North node in Pisces dreams of being left alone. He or she wants to be separated from the mass of average people so that he or she will be free to meditate or contemplate the mysteries of life. Note that they want to initiate this separation themselves; if rejection brings separation, he or she will feel trauma rather than satisfaction. This person is inhibited or shy and sometimes inclined to repress the emotions, which may be extremely difficult to express. Fussiness or quibbling supplants the desired meditation and thwarts the dream.

The nodal house positions may modify the dream. North node in the first house wants to be thought of as ambitious, energetic, and lucky. In contrast, ambitions may have been thwarted by an early marriage or an unfortunate marriage that was based more on transitory romantic feelings than real love. Feelings about relationships and life in general are changeable and often make a drain on energy, so that when opportunities arise, motivation to act on them is lacking. Sometimes there are problems from laziness or passivity.

North node in the second house wants assurance that his or her financial needs will always be met. He or she may dream of great wealth, but more commonly just wants enough to provide the basic necessities plus an allowance for indulgence in one major luxury—expensive beauty treatments, antiques, books, or whatever. (This luxury in itself doesn't seem to have any bearing on the nodal sign, it's more often connected with a rising or otherwise predominant planet). Peace and harmony are also important components of the dream. In contrast, this person is often subject to feelings of strangeness or bouts of moodiness that hinder harmony and successful attainment of dreams. It's interesting to note that there's often marked psychic ability that's repressed or totally denied. When this is channeled, moods often improve. In extreme cases, there's compulsiveness that can lead to underhanded methods of obtaining goals. Again, this sabotages the need for harmony.

North node in the third house dreams of mental vitality and of respect in some traditional field. He or she wants to be thought of as someone worth talking to. This is a person of changing interests and philosophy who's often been strongly influenced—consciously or subconsciously—by early religious, educational, or cultural dogma. These ingrained beliefs can lead to a wasting of mental ability or less traditional but nonetheless valuable talents.

North node in the fourth house wants a very loyal family and a home in which he or she will be the focal point and chief mover. Less frequently, this person dreams of developing some sort of powerful metaphysical abilities. Acknowledgement of some sort is a basic dream motif. This is a person of changing ambitions. Usually there are several career interests that are pursued in turn in an almost ruthless way. The dream of acknowledgement is often fulfilled, but the acknowledgement may not be the sort that was expected or wanted.

North node in the fifth house wants to be considered loyal, above all else. Fun, romance, and children often play a role in the dream motif. This person wants to be thought of as a powerful instrument or advocate of good. This person tends to be rather moody. He or she is inclined to attract sensitive souls to befriend; sometimes these people are cranky or difficult and severely test north node in fifth's desire to remain loyal. Parents are generally a strong influence for better or worse. Often there's over-concern about whether the parents will approve of their actions or not. If the person chooses to break away from parental dominance, he or she may suffer severe guilt pangs that hinder effective functioning. The dream of loyalty must be tempered by a primary loyalty to self before the rest of the dream can be fulfilled.

North node in the sixth house dreams of being vital, energetic, and physically and mentally healthy. They may want to be actively involved in some sort of healing art or profession. They dream of becoming psychic healers, doctors, renowned herbalists, or people noted for their healthy, attractive bodies. They dream of finding a way to take care of their body without foregoing self-indulgence and hope of being able to pass this way on to others. Sometimes mental health is emphasized rather than physical health. This person wants very much to be thought of as perceptive. He or she typically feels isolated from others and has difficulty finding emotional satisfaction. Much time is spent examining both emotions and the physical state, hoping to find a key that will allow him or her to feel more in tune with others. Self-deceit or attempts to deceive others may keep perceptions and well-being blocked or lead to misguided or self-defeating action.

North node in the seventh house dreams of gaining much through marriage and/or other relationships. He or she truly believes that teaming up with others will improve his or her lot in life. This person hopes to gain respect vicariously, through marriage or some other type of affiliation and feels that success and happiness will be guaranteed once they find their "other half"—someone who embodies those qualities he or she feels are lacking in their own make-up. This person has a great deal of sensitivity. He or she also has a great deal of psychic ability; unfortunately, both are liable to be repressed. Aggressive pursuit of an alter ego tends to drive the dream further and further out of reach until the person is forced to look within for the repressed or lacking qualities.

North node in the eighth house also hopes to realize gains through partnerships or other relationships, but the dreamed-of gains are liable to be more tangible in this case. He or she could dream of marrying a rich mate, befriending someone who dies and leaves them a sizeable inheritance, or being cut in on somebody's lottery winnings. There's a strong desire to eliminate hardship of all types. This person takes an emotional approach towards financial matters. He or she tends to spend on the basis of emotional impulse rather than need, and is often careless or impractical with money. Less frequently the person is too lavish with praise, time, or nurturing. These tendencies stem from a subconcsious feeling that he or she is incapable of amassing necessary resources without help from others.

North node in the ninth house dreams of being some type of teacher. He or she feels that education holds the key to tapping his or her fullest potentials. Success and progress are important themes of the dream motif. This person tends to let emotional factors stand in the way of success. While there may be a great amount of potential, as long as emotions take precedence over sense, the dream can't be fulfilled. Inconsistency is often a problem, since the mind rarely understands what the emotions are doing.

North node in the tenth house generally dreams of success in life. This involves overcoming limitations and rising above his or her station in life through gaining the support of authority figures or others who are in a position to help. This person tends to get trapped in a comfortable, mildly pleasant rut due to emotional ties. A parent or other family member may be instrumental in keeping the dream from being fulfilled. This usually isn't because of outright opposition; generally, it's because of subconscious fear or guilt on the part of north node in the tenth. Clannishness, bigotry, or class-consciousness can keep the person from making contacts that would be instrumental in fulfilling the dream.

· North node in the eleventh house wants some sort of a guarantee that his or her goals will be realized. He or she wants to be known as an honest person, a seeker of knowledge, and an instrument of positive change. He or she dreams of close friends to share goals with, people who will offer support without making demands. This person is typically very impressionable and not cautious enough or discriminating enough when it comes to other people. On one hand, he or she may blindly take advice without considering its source. On the other, pomposity or excessive pride may keep him or her from asking for or accepting even the most necessary or valid advice. There's a tendency to invest a great deal in emotional whims and pleasure-seeking at the expense of long-range goals.

North node in the twelfth house dreams of feeling at ease with others when in a group or one-to-one encounter, but also wants to be able to spend quite a bit of time alone. He or she wants to be something of an enigma. This person is changeable in moods and work habits. This affects his or her ability to take advantage of opportunities for dream fulfillment. While actual physical or mental health may be good, the person may allude to some mysterious tragic flaw or skeleton in the closet that prevents success. Less frequently, there's a tangible problem in this respect. The person is highly self-critical and equally critical of others, thus preventing successful interaction with others as well as with the subconscious.

Note that dreams and reality intermingle and in the process both get distorted. Reality to the client may not be reality at all, but because the client sees it as reality it becomes reality. Only the client can change this perception of reality, so the astrologer's function in interpreting the dichotomy between dreams and reality should be one of detached, objective commentator, providing the client with food for thought on the basis of what is seen in the chart. This objectivity may not be appreciated—in fact a "tell me what to do" approach may be demanded. However, with tact and patience the astrologer can point out the importance of the client making his or her own plan of action.

Most clients won't verbalize their needs in quite such a convenient way as the one we described. More likely they will be given to more matter-of-fact expressions of their dreams. As examples of this, look at these rather typical responses from clients who were asked how they'd respond to the proverbial genie if he came to grant three wishes:

North Node in Leo in the First

"More energy. Lifelong good health. A beautiful home." (A very sensitive, very talkative housewife).

North Node in Virgo in the First

"Of course, a good figure. Besides that, I'd like to go down in history as a great psychic. And I'd like to be self-sufficient in terms of the basic necessities of life." (A 27-year old language student who had recently undergone some major changes in self-awareness due to involvement in a metaphysical group).

North Node in Virgo in the Second

"More money. Advancement in my job. Success as a writer." (A real estate agent whose main hobbies are writing and fishing).

North Node in Libra in the Second

"Respect. Money. A total beauty make-over and someone to help me keep looking like that." (A philosophy and astrology student, single and living with parents).

North Node in Scorpio in the Third

"More will-power. To be able to develop my psychic abilities. Not to need tranquilizers." (A very sensitive dietician).

North Node in Sagittarius in the Third

"To be able to help my sister. To understand life. To be able to see into the future." (A newspaper employee who complained of being frequently upset and unable to make decisions).

North Node in Capricorn in the Third
"Money. Travel. A good job." (An art student who complained of being pressured, stifled, and plagued by bad luck).

North Node in Aquarius in the Third
"Travel. Not to have to work. To be an expert in something." (A political science student who dabbles in astrology).

North Node in Taurus in the Fourth
"More energy. To lose weight. To be a famous singer." (A housewife and astrology student).

North Node in Gemini in the Fourth
"More ambition. To publish a book. Lots of travel." (A philosophy and astrology student who enjoys cooking and travel).

North Node in Aries in the Fifth
"Money. To be the life of the party. To be a genius." (A salesman and father-to-be).

North Node in Taurus in the Fifth
"To be more creative. To write the Great Canadian novel. To have a greenhouse to grow exotic flowers in." (A girl who works for a pharmaceutical company, and has trouble with a domineering mother).

North Node in Gemini in the Fifth
"To make a killing on the stock market. To be able to have fun without having to worry about money. More child support from my ex-husband." (A devoted mother and astrology student, who has Uranus conjunct her south node).

North Node in Virgo in the Sixth
"Success. Good luck. Respect for my knowledge and creativity." (A talkative, nervous man who suffers from ulcers).

North Node in Libra in the Sixth
"Good luck. To meet Mr. Right. Good health." (A philosophy major).

North Node in Scorpio in the Sixth
"A good job. To understand life. To understand other people." (A music student).

North Node in Libra in the Seventh
"An active social life. To win a round-the-world cruise. To be accepted." (A man who lives a very regimented life and complained of a lack of emotional fulfillment).

North Node in Scorpio in the Seventh
"Money. Marriage. Good health." (A construction worker who was looking very hard for a potential mate).

North Node in Sagittarius in the Seventh
"A happy marriage. Education. Physical fitness." (A woman with Moon square nodes. She enjoys travel and cultural pursuits, but is generally unhappy with the quality of her life and blamed her mate for her problems).

North Node in Capricorn in the Seventh
"Someone to share my life with. Someone whom I can trust when I need advice. A yacht." (A rather plastic type who found it very difficult to accept his shortcomings, even though he admitted to being unhappy).

North Node in Virgo in the Eighth
"Privacy. Good health. To be assured I'll go to heaven." (An illegitimate child who wants to succeed as a writer).

North Node in Libra in the Eighth
"To become a good palmist. To be able to earn a living from ceramics. To become editor of Playboy." (A drifter who lost his mother at age 11. He has Sun square nodes).

North Node in Gemini in the Ninth
"To be honest no matter what. To have uninterrupted time for my studies. To invent a new form of entertainment." (A teacher who feels she learns more in school than she does through relationships).

North Node in Cancer in the Ninth
"To be a good Christian while on earth. To make my parents proud of me. To succeed as an artist." (Manager of a Christian bookstore whose religion frowns on the pursuit of higher education except in very special circumstances. Mercury is square her nodes).

North Node in Leo in the Ninth

"A measure of prominence as a teacher. To be active in government affairs. To be able to use my leadership abilities." (An English teacher and struggling writer. The Sun is square his nodes).

North Node in Aries in the Tenth

"Respect. Courage. Freedom to travel." (A social butterfly and disco habituee).

North Node in Taurus in the Tenth

"A good reputation. A PhD in English. To win the Nobel Prize for literature." (A girl who's deeply interested in astrology, philosophy and reading. She has Moon square her nodes).

North Node in Gemini in the Tenth

"The ability to attract good luck. The ability to make the most of my mind. Drama lessons." (An athlete).

North Node in Gemini in the Eleventh

"To be part of a crowd. A trip to England. To be able to create a famous character like James Bond." (A counselor who suffered a rather difficult childhood environment and an equally difficult marriage).

North Node in Cancer in the Eleventh

"The ability to lead others. To be a famous actor. To find a cure for some birth defect." (A tourist concessionaire who took over the family business rather than investing in an amateur theatre group he believed in because his parents disapproved).

North Node in Sagittarius in the Twelfth

"Money. Success in my studies. Success as a lawyer." (A student who had a rather traumatic childhood).

North Node in Capricorn in the Twelfth

"To become less vulnerable emotionally. To be in control of my situation. To be more aggressive." (A nurse).

As you can see, these capsule descriptions of dreams are full of information if you're willing to read between the lines and correlate the nodal positions. By discovering the dream, you open the door to discussion of obstacles that interfere with its fulfillment—both real obstacles and imagined ones. These can then be dealt with in a sensible way, according to the nature of the dream and the nature of the client's situation.

Certainly some dreams will be far-fetched, but to a well-trained astrologer even these will provide valuable clues about the client's needs and his ability to use nodal potential in fulfilling these needs.

Aspects to the Nodes: Choosing How to Grow

*T*o fully understand your growth pattern, you must go beyond the sign and house positions and study the aspects to the nodes.

The nature of the aspects to the nodes will tell you how easy it is for you to grow. Conjunctions to the north node seem to force you to grow, while conjunctions to the south node encourage you to do what comes naturally. Squares to the nodes reinforce the conflict of interest, causing an equal pull between wanting to grow and wanting to do what comes naturally. With squares, the involved planet invariably bears the brunt of the nodal conflict, and tends to behave in an inconsistent way. Sextiles to the north node offer opportunities for growth, while trines to the north node suggest that growth comes more easily. I use a fairly traditional orb system—nine degrees for trines, six degrees for sextiles. This means that a planet in trine to one node isn't necessarily in sextile to the other node. In other words, a trine to the north node may or may not also offer opportunities to stagnate, while a sextile to the north node invariably makes it slightly easier to stagnate.

A quincunx to the north node suggests a need for growth combined with some misconception or misperception about its results or the way of attaining it. A semi-sextile to the north node puts pressure on you to grow without making it any easier for you to do so. Semi-squares and sesquiquadrates to the north node suggest tension connected with growth. No doubt the other minor aspects give additional information, but I've as yet found no consistent way to interpret them.

Following are some typical manifestations of nodal aspects.

Sun Conjunct North Node
Seeking contact with others results in growth. Creative potential or power potential aids growth. Ability to perform on a high level in some respect stimulates growth potential.

Sun Conjunct South Node
A craving for companionship or an overwhelming need to be part of a crowd can lead to stagnation. Lack of vitality can encourage stagnation. Shyness can inhibit growth, especially if angular houses are involved.

Sun Trine North Node
A motivation to grow. A search for growth that involves seeking out people who'll encourage physical, creative or emotional development. A need to progress socially, monetarily or creatively stimulates the desire to grow.

Sun Sextile North Node
The motivation to grow is still there but you have to focus on it consciously; it doesn't come as easily as with the trine; There's a tendency to become so absorbed in some south node pursuit that you may miss opportunities to develop the north node potential. It becomes easy to let the south node keep you in a rut, although sometimes the rut is quite a pleasant one.

Sun Semi-sextile North Node
A tendency to seek an inner path to growth—meditation, spiritual studies, therapy, etc. Often the idea is to seek a passive approach to growth, although once involved the person may make great gains in spite of his or her faulty or misguided motivations. People with this aspect seem to have a high frequency of involvement in writing, healing arts, and teaching as active paths to growth. Reading, attending classes, and sometimes guru-seeking are common as passive paths.

Sun Quincunx North Node
Inhibitions make growth difficult. Sometimes there's an actual physical problem or an imagined defect that hinders growth.

Sun Semi-square, Sesquiquadrate either Node
Literal or figurative seclusion or imprisonment may encourage stagnation; these may be either self-imposed or envi-

ronmental. Often nervousness of some sort makes growth difficult.

Moon Conjunct North Node

An emotional outlook that attracts relationships that encourage growth. A need to meet people, participate in social activities, etc. stimulates awareness of the need for growth.

Moon Conjunct South Node

Often the tendency is towards griping rather than growing.

Moon Trine North Node

Feelings are allowed full expression allowing easy growth on personal and interpersonal levels. Sometimes the childhood environment offers material or less tangible advantages that make growth easier to attain.

Moon Sextile North Node

Feelings are more controlled than with the trine. Often there's a feeling of not really knowing yourself or of having to protect your "good" side from your "bad" side. There's a need to be aware of the tendency towards a stagnating, nonproductive sort of self-control.

Moon Square Nodes

The tension caused by nodal imbalance can "paralyze" the lunar potential, leaving in its place a fear of being made a fool of. Both growth and stagnation become threatening options.

Other Aspects

These seem to depend on the overall tone of the chart to a point where a general interpretation becomes almost impossible. They could have to do with cultivating qualities or experiences necessary for the fulfillment of karma, although I'd caution you to look for here-and-now interpretations before relegating all aspects in this category to the great karmic dumping-ground.

Mercury Conjunct North Node

A need to share ideas or a motivation to learn leads to growth. Learning can be either active (through doing yourself) or passive (through receiving information from others) depending on the signs involved. Angular nodes seem to incline more towards active development of growth potential regardless of the signs involved.

Mercury Conjunct South Node

Enduring may take the place of growing, since talk or planning can replace action. Pessimism may lead to a feeling that growth is impossible.

Mercury Trine North Node

This seems to be very similar to Mercury conjunct north node. An easy sociability and a need to give as well as receive put growth within close reach.

Mercury Sextile North Node

Arranging things and socializing can leave little time for personal growth, although often this person contributes to other's growth. Sometimes a one-track mind closes the door to opportunities for growth. Other times growth opportunities are seen as threats to an organized life-style.

Mercury Square Nodes

Nodal imbalance can contribute to craftiness or a tendency to use people. Often there's a tendency to chatter away about trivia to distract from the nodal imbalance. In other cases, the square operates much like Mercury conjunct south node.

Other Aspects

These vary in effect from a compulsion to tell others about your troubles whether they want to hear about them or not, to a need to avoid others who don't share your feelings, to an active cultivation of beneficial or repressive social activities or contacts.

Venus Conjunct North Node

Generally this person expresses his or her growth potential in a charming, easy-to-take way. Sociability aids growth.

Venus Conjunct South Node

This person may have trouble adapting to new people and circumstances. Often there's difficulty in close relationships. The person may be agreeable enough but about the wrong things. Sometimes an over-developed sense of duty contributes to emotional stagnation.

Venus Trine North Node

Romance, marriage can set the stage for growth. There's an attraction to artistic, friendly, or loving people that aids growth. Otherwise very much like Venus conjunct north node.

Venus Sextile North Node

Making sacrifices for others may either provide opportunities for growth or contribute to personal stagnation, depending on how the person chooses to handle the nodal potentials.

Venus Square Nodes

Laziness can become a means of coping with nodal imbalance. Dissatisfaction at the nodal and Venus locations is common. Venus conjunct south node tendencies may be displayed. This aspect seems to have a high incidence in charts of people who come from broken homes or have a history of romantic difficulties.

Other Aspects

These vary in effect from excessive or inappropriate demonstrativeness to a compulsion to bore others with your romantic problems, to lack of discrimination about contacts made. Less frequently demonstrativeness or friendliness are inhibited.

Mars Conjunct North Node

Assertiveness leads to growth, although during the overcompensating phase of the nodal balancing act assertiveness can get out of hand and lead to quarrels. Ability to concentrate on whatever goal is represented enhances growth potential. A need for activity stimulates growth.

Mars Conjunct South Node

Adaptability is limited, hindering growth. A tendency towards accident-proneness or fear of injury can lead to stagnation. When angular this position frequently coincides with loss of a mate or parent through death or separation or sometimes some traumatic blow to the self-esteem at an early age.

Mars Trine North Node

Ability to face potentially dangerous situations and a great deal of courage are generally growth–enhancing assets. A need to cooperate with others encourages growth. A need for healthy sex or a desire for children can stimulate growth.

Mars Sextile North Node

Adaptability must be consciously worked at if growth is to come. Energy is more easily channeled into resisting growth than seeking it. The more the person consciously channels his or her energy into growth-producing activities, the more difficulties that will be overcome.

Mars Square Nodes

This person generally wants to grow and starts new activities accordingly but may lose interest in growing once challenges have to be faced; the nodal pull can exert tremendous tension. There's similarity with Mars conjunct north node in that tensions caused by the nodal imbalance often find an outlet in quarreling or aggressiveness; there are also many similarities to Mars conjunct south node. The way in which conflicts are dealt with will tell you a great deal about the state of nodal balance.

Mars Semi-sextile North Node

Marriage, sexual encounters, and other relationships often provide opportunities for growth although these are sometimes misconstructed in some way and seen as attempts by the other party to repress the person or alter his or her growth pattern.

Mars Semi-square North Node

Bad news, mourning of some sort, or destructive behavior on the part of the person or someone in his or her circle may inhibit growth at times.

Mars Sesquiquadrate North Node

Growth potential is inhibited or tends to fluctuate due to unhealthy environmental circumstances. If nodes are succedent, growth may be interfered with through circumstances beyond the person's control or destructive behavior on the person's part. If nodes are cadent, fatalism and a tendency to grin (or gripe) and bear things may inhibit growth. Mourning over a death or other type of loss may interfere with growth.

Other Aspects

Must be interpreted according to the overall tone of the chart. The quincunx to the north node seems to coincide often with complaints of being smothered or stifled in some way.

Jupiter Conjunct North Node

Good companionship is conducive to growth. Often growth is linked to teaching, community work or some kind of adventuring.

Jupiter Conjunct South Node

Misguided religious, expansive, or revolutionary tendencies can impede growth. Sociability sometimes detracts from the growth process. Growth can be attained by consciously working on it, but often inner growth is confused with status or material progress.

Jupiter Trine North Node

Much like Jupiter conjunct north node. Ability to get along easily with others makes growth an instinctive process.

Jupiter Sextile North Node

Adaptability comes more easily than growth. A need for material growth or progress may override the need for inner growth. Moodiness or maladjustment may cause opportunities for growth to be overlooked or ignored.

Jupiter Square Nodes

The tensions caused by the nodal imbalance can trigger religious fanaticism, extravagance, and bandwagon-jumping along similar lines to Jupiter conjunct south node. A tendency to play both ends against the middle is commonly employed as a coping mechanism; other times there's a "What's in it for me?" approach. Note the tactics used to gain material or relationship advantages; this will tell you a great deal about nodal balance. It's very common for the person to complain of bad luck in romance or just plain all-around bad luck.

Jupiter Semi-sextile North Node

This seems to operate much like the sextile with an added inclination to withdraw when pushed. Sociability and moods tend to be erratic.

Jupiter Quincunx North Node

Awareness of growth potential is erratic, subject to sudden blocks or repression offset by occasional periods of heightened awareness; sometimes this is due to an illness or an excess—smoking, drinking, overeating, etc. Health seems to be most likely to suffer if the nodes are cadent; the person may complain he or she is drowning, smothering, or being otherwise overwhelmed by environmental conditions. Argumentativeness and "full of hot air" tendencies are often employed as coping mechanisms.

Other Aspects

Must be judged on the basis of the overall tone of the chart.

Saturn Conjunct North Node

Ability to achieve growth by working at it. During the overcompensating phase of nodal balance moodiness may be a problem. Sometimes there's a physical problem involving the nodal polarity that must be overcome. This person is often a loner and is happiest when able to have time alone to reflect on how he or she is to achieve his or her goals.

Saturn Conjunct South Node

Growth may trigger feelings of not fitting in or being out of touch; conformity may lead to stagnation. There's a strong feeling of something missing within the person, leading to dissatisfaction with relationships and circumstances. As with Saturn conjunct the north node, there may be an illness connected with the nodal polarity. The tendency is to try to repress awareness of the need for growth.

Saturn Trine North Node

A need for material progress stimulates a desire for growth. Patience and ability to tolerate seclusion are conducive to growth. In other respects, much like Saturn conjunct north node.

Saturn Sextile North Node

Upbringing seems to play a major role in the interpretation of this aspect. If the person has been left in a comfortable position by parents or other benefactors, opportunities for growth may be rejected. Even when birth conditions don't leave opportunities to rest on the family laurels, growth may be considered only within the narrow limits of what's acceptable by family or parental standards. Growth potential may be damaged or repressed as a result of guilt feelings or arguments.

Saturn Square Nodes

Much like Saturn conjunct south node. Pessimism is one manifestation of the nodal conflict; this must be consciously dealt with and eradicated if growth is to take place.

Other aspects

These vary in effect from stimulating an endless search for variety to triggering a craving for solitude or an unvarying routine. They can either help or hinder growth depending on the overall tone of the chart.

Uranus Conjunct North Node

An attraction towards the unusual contributes to growth. There's a bit of the adventurer in this person, so when over-compensation takes place, impulsiveness and sensation-seeking can bring problems. When the nodes are balanced, these tendencies are often channeled into the study of patterns, music, science, ecology, etc.

Uranus Conjunct South Node

The tendency is towards drastic action. A craving for a position of power or authority can also show up. A desire to live a totally unrestricted life can contribute to stagnation since lack of discipline or responsibility can limit growth potential.

Uranus Trine North Node

Very much like Uranus conjunct north node. Best opportunities for growth can be found in humanitarian pursuits. A need to share new and varied experiences with others is conducive to growth.

Uranus Sextile North Node

A search for paths to change can offer many opportunities for growth, but the temptation is to substitute searching for growing which means that the person often gets change without the benefit of progress. Impulsiveness in relationships can hinder growth. A need to share experiences with others can lead to an emphasis on joining instead of growing.

Uranus Square Nodes

The tensions caused by nodal imbalance can lead to upsetting experiences involving group or individual relationship or circumstances in general. A craving for independence can cause sudden setbacks in terms of growth or lead to an improper channeling of growth potential. Sometimes this person is inclined to stick to his or her guns out of sheer contrariness; other times the principle of being entitled to one's opinion seems to matter more than the rightness or wrongness of the opinion. Arguing provides an outlet for the inner tension.

Uranus Semi-sextile North Node

An almost instinctive ability to make "lucky" decisions does little to instill a motivation towards conscious growth. Relationships and commitments seem to play a role in the circumstances surrounding growth. These may offer some opportunities while denying others that the person might possibly prefer.

Other Aspects

These vary in effect but have in common a certain flashiness. Sudden displays of enthusiasm or temper are often outlets for tension. There's a tendency to get excited rather easily. Sudden cravings for influence over others can be mistaken for growth needs, and a sense of frustration often is felt when things don't work out as conceived.

Neptune Conjunct North Node

Sensitivity enhances growth potential. There's a tendency to seek the impossible or the ideal that keeps the person aiming higher and higher. In the over-compensation phase, there can be problems stemming from anti-social behavior, avoidance of people, escapist tendencies and use of consciousness-altering substances are also common.

Neptune Conjunct South Node

A peculairity or confused issue may encourage stagnation. Sometimes there's a medical disorder, a drinking problem, or a weight problem; other times inhibitions or misperceptions hinder growth.

Neptune Trine North Node

Much like north node conjunct Neptune. There's a tendency to expect more than is actually possible from individuals, institutions, or society in general; in the overcompensation phase this can trigger problems. There's an enjoyment of growth and of helping others to grow.

Neptune Sextile North Node

A readiness to sacrifice can contribute to stagnation. Plans are carried out in a more methodical way with less striving for new heights. Growth is a slow process, sometimes involving intense suffering or guilt pangs about leaving the comfortable rut behind; rejecting opportunities for growth may hold the person back.

Neptune Square Nodes

Similar to Neptune conjuct the south node. The tension produced by the nodal imbalance may trigger a tendency to exploit others. "Bad luck" or disappointments involving Neptune's sign and/or house position are frequently mentioned.

Other Aspects

These vary in effect. They often seem to lessen adaptability and contribute to discord in work or relationships. Emotional problems or inhibitions connected with interpersonal dealings are commonly displayed.

Pluto Conjunct North Node

The person often seems to be forced to take some sort of separative or eliminative action in order to grow. Relationships with groups or individuals seem to play a major role in the growth process. Leadership abilities enhance growth.

Pluto Conjunct South Node

This person is often affected by violence, which hinders growth. Mass destiny, upheavals, destructive or self-destructive behavior can be stumbling-blocks. Separation of some sort, violence, and, less frequently, escapism may impede growth. Circumstances beyond control or perhaps karma could make it necessary to constantly fight against stagnation.

Pluto Trine North Node

This person generally feels a need to seek people or experiences that will aid growth. Sometimes there's a desire to be a public figure of some sort; this can spur the person onwards towards growth. Again relationships seem to play a major role in growth. Often the person instinctively knows which relationship will provide growth opportunities and which will offer stagnation.

Pluto Sextile North Node

Here there's ability to make tremendous efforts towards growth and ability to perform very difficult tasks by using all available discipline. Yet opportunities for growth may not be taken and these abilities may lie dormant. Often the person participates in group or mass goal achievement to the detriment of personal growth.

Pluto Square Nodes

Depending on how this is being used, it takes on the nature of one of the Pluto-node conjunctions. The person often complains that relationships are a burden or feels that individuals or society as a whole are cramping his or her style. Tensions caused by the nodal imbalance can contribute to fanaticism or lead to pursuit of unwise goals. In extreme cases there may be a compulsion to exploit others or rid them of some attitudes that the individual sees as unhealthy or abnormal. A craving for power may lead to problems or feelings of frustration.

Other aspects

These vary in effect from a strong need to get your own way to outright ruthlessness. Occasionally the person feels emotionally repressed or feels that growth is being inhibited by a person or by society as a whole. A need to dominate others either intellectually or physically is sometimes felt. This can lead to either growth or frustration, depending on how it's handled.

North Node Conjunct Midheaven

A need for one-to-one relationships stimulates growth. Optimism aids growth potential.

South Node Conjunct Midheaven
Inhibitions encourage stagnation.

North Node Trine Midheaven
Similar to north node conjunct midheaven, except that the need is to find like-minded people. There's also a greater emphasis on gaining a deeper understanding of the workings of relationships in order to facilitate growth. Relationships tend to be made for the purpose of reaching joint goals or sharing growth gains.

North Node Sextile Midheaven
Similar to south node conjunct midheaven. There's a tendency to be so occupied with the inner-self and its workings that opportunities for growth may be missed. It's usually necessary to struggle with some sort of house-related difficulties before opportunities for growth can be taken advantage of.

Nodes Square Midheaven
There's a tendency not to fit into the environment, to feel odd, be odd, or to be misunderstood. As a result, difficulties arise frequently in the course of activities involving others, particularly those which involve sharing or teamwork. There's still ability to grow and progress, and often the tension generated by the nodal conflict actually triggers growth, but there may be many hassles with parents or authority figures over the type of growth desired or the means of attaining it.

Other Aspects
These vary in effect but usually over-emphasize one facet of a relationship. Sometimes relationships are based strictly on shared interests with the emotions being kept totally out of the picture. Other times, feelings play the major role in relationships and group activities while other types of sharing are given short shrift. Occasionally the person feels a compulsion to bare his or her soul to anyone who will listen.

North Node Conjunct Ascendant
Ability to get along well with others enhances growth potential. Charming self-projection encourages growth-contacts.

South Node Conjunct Ascendant
A tendency to feel inhibited can encourage stagnation.

North Node Trine Ascendant
Sharing interests with like-minded people makes it easier to grow. There's a tendency to enter into relationships that prove to be profitable from a growth standpoint. Creation of a beautiful environment within or without leads to growth in other areas.

North Node Sextile Ascendant
Experiences gained in the involved houses often encourages stagnation. There's often a pattern of early responsibilities where maturity is expected of one too young to understand the need or else a longer-than-average childhood.

Nodes Square Ascendant
The tension produced by the nodal conflict can lead to either a discordant sort of self-projection or a tendency to attract discordant people. A tendency towards clannishness or social climbing can contribute to stagnation.

Other Aspects.
These vary, but give some sort of craving for a particular type of relationship as a rule. Sometimes there's an emphasis on superficial social contacts, the "lots of acquaintances, but no friends" syndrome. Other times there's a craving for a soulmate or alter ego.

Taking nodal positions and aspects out of context, breaking them down, giving interpretations for each mode of their functioning serves a useful purpose, for it enables you to see where certain patterns or tendencies come from. However, there's one problem with interpretations of this sort—they leave the hardest part of the work undone. I'm of course referring to the synthesis of the nodes. I've stressed throughout this book that any interpretations given here should be taken as starting points. Your job as an astrologer is to fill in the blanks I've left by understanding the "feel" of each position and then reading between the lines and modifying your interpretation to fit the individual. This is something that no book can teach. Only practice with charts familiar to you can give you the experience in synthesis that's necessary for good interpretation.

Antidotes for Nodal Imbalance

So far we've been stressing the negative—the problems and symptoms of nodal imbalance. This has been necessary in order to know exactly what we're dealing with. But we'd be remiss to end our discussion without offering solutions to the problems presented.

The antidotes have been grouped according to the type of imbalance. For example, north node in Aries, north node in the first house, and tension–producing aspects between Mars and the nodes are all listed under "Aries Imbalance". To choose the best antidote, you'll have to take the whole nodal configuration into account.

Antidotes for Aries Imbalance

Psychological counselling (particularly assertiveness training) is often helpful in learning to utilize the Aries north node. The client might be advised to write or tape a statement of his or her philosophy of life, including a list of goals for the next year. You may then help the client determine how to best express this philosophy while fulfilling the goals. Scientific study, particularly in the field of physics or physical development, may be recommended if the client shows aptitude along these lines. Any sort of discipline program—from Scouting to the National Guards—could prove beneficial. Travel—preferably alone—is recommended. Leadership roles—particularly in the work sphere, should be accepted.

For any type of Aries imbalance, the catch-phrase should be "Try something new." This "something new" should naturally coincide with some untapped talent, as shown in the chart.

For many reasons, clients may not be ready to embark on a totally new life style. In these cases, a new hobby could prove beneficial. Among the hobbies I'd recommend for Aries nodal imbalance are: any sort of nature activities from hunting to photographing wildlife, football or soccer, hockey, boxing or karate, enamel work.

Antidotes for Taurus Imbalance

Gardening seems to be a particularly good antidote for the impracticality that often accompanies an underdeveloped north node in Taurus. Cooking courses often prove helpful. The client should be encouraged to sing and listen to music. If manual dexterity is shown in the chart, the client should be encouraged to use it in making things. If there's no manual dexterity shown, the client could be encouraged to build-up a collection of something—biographies, novels, gadgets, etc.—in an area of interest. Flower arranging could prove to be a useful antidote.

The client should be encouraged to avoid rushing and activities that create momentary excitement without contributing to future security.

North node in Taurus often has untapped artistic potential. Music, sewing, and painting are excellent outlets for these. And north node in the second house, when undeveloped, often speaks of a latent talent that could be used to bring in money or other resources. These avenues should be fully explored with the client.

Antidotes for Gemini Imbalance

The client should be encouraged to keep a diary. If the client has knowledge to share, he or she should be encouraged to do so through teaching, writing, correspondence, or whatever way is most convenient. Travel in moderation often proves beneficial. Involvement in civil rights or community improvement causes can be helpful. The imagination should be tapped so that creativity can be developed and put to use in strategy—planning, writing, photography, or some other area according to the chart. If the client is amenable to a career change or program of career training, there are many obvious choices that would encourage development of the north node. Among these are: journalism, newspaper work, radio work, television work, fiction writing, Air Force career, electrical work, reporting, and linguistics. Dancing could be a possibility, although unless the client is very young or has prior training this would probably be better as a hobby choice than as a career choice.

The client should be encouraged to steer clear of tiring or repetitive routines that don't provide opportunities to develop adaptability. At the same time, he must be discouraged from the "Jack of all trades, master of none" syndrome. If there are signs of perpetual studentism, the client should be encouraged to start doing something with his present store of knowledge before trying to gain more.

Hobbies should stress physical agility and manual dexterity. Origami, mobile-making, collage-making and the like are recommended. For the more active, fencing, tennis, golf, and dancing are good choices.

Antidotes for Cancer Imbalance

If career advice is sought, the client should be steered into a nurturing profession. Nursing, acting, dressmaking, pilot or stewardess, gynecology or child care would be logical choices if other areas of the chart are in agreement. Creativity should be channeled. Painting, interior decorating, weaving, and poetry-writing are particularly recommended. In cases where the north node has been repressed to the point of blockage, psychodrama could prove helpful. If the client has adequate understanding of astrology, a dramatization of the nodal dialogues (or the troublesome nodal configuration) could be beneficial, provided you feel comfortable about this technique yourself.

A thorough health check-up should be advised if the client complains of lethargy or any other physical symptoms, since health problems seem to be slightly more frequent than normal with these placings. Both reading and writing can be beneficial antidotes. The Cancer need to protect and nurture must be satisfied. Housekeeping can often prove to be an effective antidote, as can anything connected with land maintenance. History and genealogy often satisfy the north node's need to preserve and protect. On another level, swimming, calisthenics, or yoga could appeal by giving the client a feeling of doing something beneficial in terms of self-preservation.

Antidotes for Leo Imbalance

As with Cancer, psychodrama or dramatization of the nodal dilemma can be helpful if the repression is severe. Interior decorating, set design, etc. can be excellent antidotes if there's aptitude in these directions. Political involvement and involvement in community action programs are ideal for stimulating a sluggish node in this position. The client should be encouraged to accept leadership roles in any capacity for which he's suited.

The client should be engaged in a "What would happen if . . ." dialogue in which he or she is asked to visualize the worst possible things that could result from developing the north node. You should then help the client deal with these fears. This technique works best with clients who are able to laugh at themselves, since it's often necessary to point out the preposterousness of his or her fears.

You should make certain that the client hasn't confused ambition with ruthlessness, since this seems to be a frequent misconception with both Aquarius south node and north node in the fifth house. It seems to be less common with Sun square nodes, et al, although it sometimes manifests here as well.

Antidotes for Virgo Imbalance

Typing is a very helpful antidote, since it encourages neatness and order. The study of history is recommended if there's aptitude along these lines. Gardening is a very good antidote. Writing should be encouraged, with inspirational writing, social commentary, and ideas stressing reform being especially good. Public speaking should also be encouraged, with literary, analytical, scientific, and gardening topics being favored. Should there be no aptitude along these lines, an alternative topic should be sought according to the overall chart.

If career advice is sought, secretarial work is an obvious choice; however few male clients are likely to find this attractive, no matter how much aptitude they have. Other good choices would be bookbinding, statistical work, historical work, work in a stationery store, and writing of any type. If the client is young enough and capable of receiving proper training, law or paralegal work might be considered. Again you'd want to look for additional corroboration from the rest of the chart.

When north node is in Virgo in the twelfth or first house, north node is in Aries in the sixth or seventh house, or Mercury is squaring the nodes from the sixth, seventh, twelfth, or first houses, there are usually problems connected with a low self-image or a negative outlook on life. There's also often a history of restriction of some sort. In these cases, it would be a good idea to suggest professional counselling if the problems are severe. Reading such as *I'm OK—You're OK*, Assagioli's writings, and much of the literature on Gestalt Therapy (especially Fritz Perls' writings) might also be helpful.

Certain hobbies could prove to be both enjoyable and beneficial as antidotes. Among these are music, bicycling, walking, and many types of volunteer work. Crafts of various types might also be considered if according to the client's aptitudes. It's common for clients in these categories to have no idea what they might be interested in—let alone good at—so you should be prepared to spend a fair amount of time exploring along these lines.

Antidotes for Libra Imbalance

The client should be advised to get a complete beauty treatment, including new hair style, in preparation for developing a new lifestyle. Even men can benefit from a new hairstyle. Likewise, shopping for a new wardrobe or new furnishings can be a beneficial antidote, as any purchase would tend to remind the client that a new lifestyle is beginning. For best results, color selection should be geared to the imbalance. Dancing is a good antidote. If the client has any physical symptoms, a medical check-up should be advised, since this is another one of the imbalances that's most capable of triggering illness. Boating, cruises, and water sports can be helpful antidotes.

The client should be advised to consciously seek out activities that stress partnership and teamwork, rather than trying to do everything himself or herself.

If career advice is sought, the following could be recommended if other factors in the chart show aptitude: hairdresser or barber, artist, interior decorator, lawyer, stewardess or pilot.

Antidotes för Scorpio Imbalance

These seem to be the most subconscious of all imbalances, and client awareness is often very limited unless he or she is in a rather painful situation. Unless the client is receptive to what you say, you may not have much luck. Even if the client is receptive, these types of imbalances often need psychological counselling before they can be alleviated, due to their strong fixed overtones.

The study of mysticism can be a beneficial antidote if the client is relatively level-headed. Rosicrucianism, Huna, the Edgar Cayce readings, the Seth readings, astrology, palmistry or graphology would be safe suggestions. Scientific studies such as chemistry can also be beneficial. For some clients, perfume-making will appeal. Philosophy is another good antidote. The particular philosophy would of course depend on the client's aptitudes and interests. Research work of any type would prove beneficial. The client will be happiest doing something that he or she feels will have important results. Hobbies are less effective for these clients than for most unless they involve serious study. Study and research are the best antidotes for these imbalances provided the client has sufficient intelligence and powers of concentration, since this type of antidote requires minimal risk-taking and only a modest cash outlay. The client should be referred to the appropriate study and research groups since, as with Libra, teamwork is an important factor in balancing.

Antidotes for Sagittarius Imbalance

The client should be encouraged to share any specialized knowledge he or she has, either by teaching or through other means—writing, public speaking, etc. As with Scorpio, the study of philosophy is a beneficial antidote. Religious studies could also prove helpful. The client's intuition should be developed and given a positive outlet. Dream study, astrology, palmistry, graphology and many branches of parapsychology could prove useful outlets, although you should be very certain that the client is level-headed enough to use these properly. Travel is often a beneficial antidote. Work involving giving tourists various types of information (i.e. tour guide, travel agent, hotel information desk, etc.) could be quite rewarding.

Sports can be good antidotes. High jumping, rope jumping, walking, running, jogging, or any other type of physical exercise for which aptitude is shown could be recommended. It sometimes happens that the client is for one reason or another stuck in a dull, routine job—clerical, assembly line, switchboard, etc. If there's no way out of the job due to the client's age and economic needs, it's crucial to expand the sphere of after-work activities.

If career advice is sought, challenge should be the primary quality stressed. According to the client's aptitudes, consider the following options: adult education, lecturer (with philosophy, law, and civil rights being ideal areas), priest, minister, rabbi, nun, doctor, nurse, paramedic, inspector, proofreader, publisher, missionary, evangelist, salesperson. The client should be encouraged to free himself or herself from stagnant ties where possible. At the same time, he or she should be discouraged from drifting or living totally on an intellectual plane. Sometimes pet ownership can provide a helpful counter-balance for these tendencies.

Antidotes for Capricorn Imbalance

Mathematical work can be an excellent antidote. To a lesser extent, astrology and numerology can be helpful. The client must be encouraged to take responsibility for his or her own life rather than blaming parents, superiors, or others for his or her problems. Boating and water sports can sometimes be beneficial antidotes. Leadership roles should be taken where possible. Those that provide titles (chairperson, president, etc.) are especially good for enhancing self-esteem, which is usually lacking. Activities that stress discipline and strategy are particularly good. Among these would be chess, yoga, National Guards, etc. The need for security must be fulfilled.

Occasionally the client will have no ambition to do anything about the imbalance, in spite of complaints about the quality of life. These imbalances seem to be particularly fond of illogical Yeah-But dialogues. In cases where the client insists that you must "solve" his or her problem single-handedly, you can do very little but stress the fact that astrology teaches self-responsibility and suggest that the client come back when he or she is ready to accept this tenet or find another astrologer.

Psychological counselling might also be recommended: this should be of a type that stresses a "here-and-now" approach.

Antidote for Aquarius Imbalance

Any type of scientific study for which the client shows aptitude would be a good antidote. Public speaking should be encouraged, with history, literature, art, and opinion being good areas to explore. Writing is an excellent antidote, with the areas of law, cultures and astrology being ideal if there's aptitude in this direction. Poetry is also a good choice. Music—both playing and listening—can be very helpful. Naturally, astrology will come to your mind as an antidote. It can be a good one provided the client has the aptitude and motivation necessary for its proper use. Independence should be encouraged.

These clients must be made aware of the potentials they were born with, since many are inclined to feel they have only one talent and can become very discouraged if circumstances close doors or block paths in that direction. Fixity must be dealt with positively. The client must be made aware of his or her untapped originality and be encouraged to use it.

Antidotes for Pisces Imbalance

Psychodrama can be a useful tool in unlocking nodal potential. Education in keeping with the client's aptitudes is recommended, with literature, geography and medicine being ideal choices where aptitude permits. Fishing and other water sports often prove beneficial. Public speaking should be encouraged. If aptitude is shown, magic or creating illusions, painting, sculpture, boating or water sports could be a good topic. Writing is also good particularly in the areas of astronomy, myths or legends, poetry, instructional material, nurturing themes, and medicine. Hypnotism might be another good choice if the client can gain sufficient knowledge in this field.

Unless the overall tone of the chart is contradictory, the client should be discouraged from entering any profession where the overall emphasis is on strict discipline or nit-picking, since this would reinforce the very tendencies that need to be softened or balanced. Discipline can be given a bit more emphasis if the client is operating in an entertainment capacity. Some good career choices would be: sales, cooking, acrobatics, gymnastics, detective work, painting and design. Generally the clients I've met with these types of imbalance have been hard workers—close to workaholics in some cases. Usually they need relaxation more than work motivation. If the client is in a high-pressure job or required to work long hours, it's important that the antidote be something that's done for the love of it and is conducive to relaxation. Religious and spiritual activities often prove to be helpful antidotes. Many clients who remain unmoved by other options will be drawn to these.

The theory behind these antidotes is that they draw out the untapped or misused potential in a positive way, thus opening the door for further unlocking of nodal potential. Even something as simple as going to a movie or play (north node in Aries, Leo, Cancer, Pisces, fourth, fifth, twelfth, Sun, Moon, or Neptune interfering with nodal balance) can subconsciously stimulate a need to explore or channel the unused or misused potential. Once this need is felt, the client will understand the results of nodal imbalance and will be better able to correct it.

Another type of antidote I sometimes suggest is the color antidote. This is very easy to use and requires minimal effort on the client's chart. It involves wearing a color that will stimulate latent or weak qualities that need to be developed. Like the other antidotes mentioned, colors help trigger a subconscious awareness of potential, which makes this potential easier to develop on a conscious level. I also suspect that color antidotes can be helpful in making others more receptive to the change the client is trying to effect. In other words, those dealing with the client will be more motivated to accept the client's new mode of self-expression.

I use the following color antidotes:

Bright Red

For stimulating enterprise, interest in growth, and need for accomplishment; to stimulate north node in Aries.

Pink

For stimulating practicality, interest in growth, and self-discipline; to stimulate north node in Taurus.

Patterns with a heavy emphasis on purple

For stimulating adaptability, exploration, and mental tranquility; to stimulate Gemini north node.

Smoky colors (especially gray)

For encouraging kindness, concern with growth, and a more realistic attitude towards life; to stimulate north node in Cancer.

Gold or yellow

To encourage the client to live and let live, stimulate powers of persuasion, encourage self-sufficiency and pride; to stimulate north node in Leo.

Navy blue

To stimulate powers of discrimination, learning ability, and fulfillment of potentials; to stimulate north node in Virgo.

Pale blue

To stimulate charm, sense of humor and productivity; to stimulate north node in Libra.

Dark red

To stimulate powers of discernment, to increase ability to get along with others, interest in growth, and objectivity, to foster belief in self and others; to stimulate north node in Scorpio.

Purple

To stimulate sense of humor, reserve, reliability; to stimulate north node in Sagittarius.

Black

To stimulate reliability and stability, to channel love into positive paths of expression; to stimulate north node in Capricorn.

Bright blue

To stimulate humanitarianism, to increase awareness of need for rewarding activities, to encourage change; to stimulate north node in Aquarius.

Soft greens (especially sea-green)

To stimulate humility, productivity, and adaptability; to stimulate north node in Pisces.

Bright red

Stimulates a sluggish north node in the first house, helps attract publicity for the client and encourages conservatism.

Red-orange

Stimulates north node in the second house; encourages prudence and the development of meaningful values.

Orange

Stimulates north node in the third house and encourages caution.

Orange-yellow

Stimulates north node in the fourth house; encourages prudence, self-control and positive self-restraint, and discourages gambling.

Yellow

Stimulates a sluggish north node in the fifth house. In addition to the effects previously mentioned, it can encourage fidelity.

Yellow-green

A beneficial stimulant for sixth house north node; can stimulate self-expression abilities.

Bright green

Encourages harmony in romance, marriage, and partnerships, stimulates north node in the seventh house.

Green blue

Encourages inner contentment in a positive way, caution in financial transactions and other types of barter, prudence; stimulates north node in the eighth house; encourages self-control and discourages overspending and overinvesting.

Pure blue and purple

Both seem to be effective in stimulating a sluggish north node in the ninth house. A small piece of jewelry set with a topaz can also be effective. The topaz may also stimulate latent powers of persuasion.

Indigo

Stimulates north node in the tenth house; encourages persistence, and can assist in attempts to gain harmony in relationships with superiors and parents. It can also be beneficial to clients who are striving for more vocational stability. In addition, it can stimulate enthusiasm for work and living in general.

Violet

Encourages enthusiasm and stimulates north node in the eleventh house.

Violet red

Encourages self-expression and honesty; stimulates north node in the twelfth house.

When the Sun is interfering with nodal balance, the client lacks either the confidence or the energy necessary to grow. A strong dose of yellow can provide assistance in these respects, especially when Sun is conjunct the south node or squaring the nodes from an angular house.

With the Moon contributing to the nodal imbalance, sensitivity and adaptability are often blocked or misdirected. Relationship problems, "doormatitis", and martyr tendencies are also common. In these cases, the best color antidotes are white or indigo.

If Mercury is interfering with nodal balance, productivity may be affected. There's also a tendency to neglect or misuse the mental abilities—especially in the case of Mercury square nodes. Gray and violet are often effective antidotes, but for best results the client should also be advised to write, keep a diary, study astrology, or engage in some other type of activity that will foster self-awareness.

When Venus is interfering with nodal balance, there's usually a search for something which is never quite successful due to insufficient quality or quantity.Venusian skills—

gardening, cooking, flower-arranging, financial skill, self-enhancement, designing, hair care, etc.—are often under-developed. A pessimistic outlook on life is frequent, particularly with the square. Green can be an effective antidote for these problems, particularly when used in home decorating.

An obstreperous Mars can trigger trouble even when it doesn't interfere with the nodes. When it contributes to nodal imbalance, it encourages hyperactivity and can block or pervert ambitions. It can also inhibit kindness. Red or orange can work well as antidotes, particularly when north node or Mars is in Aries, the first house, or the twelfth house conjunct the ascendant. In these cases, red acts as a personal stop sign; whenever the client catches sight of it he or she gets a subconscious reminder to slow down.

When Jupiter is interfering with nodal balance, progress and growth are often bottled up on the inner level. Attempts at growth can be frustrated or stifled by obstacles or the need for accomplishments and progress can be totally ignored for one reason or another. Red and blue are the most effective color antidotes and are especially useful in cases with Jupiter conjunct the south node or Jupiter squaring the nodes from an angular house.

Black and blue both stimulate latent Saturnian abilities—math skills, political skills, proper posture and movement, etc. When Saturn interferes with nodal balance sociability is often adversely affected. Concentration may become very difficult as well—particularly when Saturn is conjunct the south node or when Saturn is squaring the nodes from an angular house. Black and blue are both helpful in these cases.

When Uranus is interfering with nodal balance, it can put a damper on your creativity or your intellectual abilities. It may also inhibit cooperation or give you trouble in dealings with authority figures or the establishment. Light browns and whites are intellectually stimulating and can be good antidotes for these problems. When I'm stymied by a chart or suffering from writer's block, I frequently change into an old beige T-shirt, and in about 10 minutes I always find that my "block" is gone. I picked up this trick after noticing that on beige T-shirt days I was invariably drawn to writing and intellectual activities—often to the point where my housework was sadly neglected. I now try to wear white or put on a pair of jeans (preferably not too faded) on days when housework has top priority. (My Uranus is trine my south node.)

Dull gray and "silvered" tones counteract negative Neptune interference by encouraging alertness, decreasing tendencies toward lying, gullibility, self-deception, and thoughtlessness. A large piece of agate—as a touchstone or in jewelry—or a ring or pendant set with a moonstone or opal may also prove to be an effective antidote, particularly in cases of Neptune squaring the nodes from an angular house or conjunct the south node.

Constant, disruptive change is common when Pluto interferes with nodal balance. Lack of consideration or deliberation can also be a problem. Dark brown and black are effective antidotes.

Note that the color antidotes are not specifically geared to the nodes alone. They may also be used for any planet in difficulty. For example, my Pluto, although it trines my north node, is in a challenging T-square involving Mercury and my Moon. This often causes me writing difficulties, particularly when it comes to things ilke footnotes, bibliographies, and rewrites. If I know I have to tackle something along these lines, I try to wear something dark brown. I find that this helps me keep control of my topic and tones down my impatience with having to redo things.

I realize that some of you will dismiss the color antidote theory as so much mystical balderdash. That's OK—if it doesn't work for you or doesn't appeal to you, by all means disregard it. But before you dismiss it, try it on yourself or get someone objective to try it. You may be surprised!

Before leaving the topic of antidotes, I'd like to mention in passing that I strongly suspect that certain types of music can be effective antidotes for nodal imbalance. I'm presently studying musical correlations to astrological patterns and would suggest that those of you interested in music as a therapeutic measure do likewise.

In "prescribing" any antidote, you must consider:
1. The client's age, sex and overall physical state.
2. The client's attitude towards each potential antidote.
    An appealing antidote should always be favored over

one that's met with disapproval or apathy, since motivation is a crucial factor.

3. The client's stability level. Clients with severe problems should be referred to the proper specialists— psychologists, financial advisors, or experts in their field who might be more competent than you in their particular area. There are some problems that astrologers shouldn't even attempt to tackle without proper non-astrological training.

4. The client's social and economic circumstances.

5. The client's past training and accomplishments and his or her present type of employment.

Many astrologers seem to be looking for pat answers. ("Ah yes, a neglected Leo north node in the ninth house. . . . Find yourself a drama coach my dear and then hightail it to Hollywood!") Clients encourage this search, because many prefer to have someone find the answer for them. But there are no hard and fast rules, and no pat answers. As an astrologer, your job is to come up with workable options. But only the client can decide which options to accept or reject. Astrologers who lead their clients to believe otherwise or succumb to client's pressure to take responsibility for their lives by making their decisions for them are playing a dangerous and destructive role which can only result in personal dissatisfaction and client badmouthing at best.

Additional Sources of Information

On the Nodes:

Cunningham, Donna, *An Astrological Guide to Self-Awareness,* California: CRCS 1978

Dobyns, Zipporah, *The Node Book,* California: TIA 1973

Grebner, Bernice, *Lunar Nodes,* Illinois: Bernice Grebner 1973

Hickey, Isabel, *Astrology: A Cosmic Science,* Massachusetts: Isabel Hickey 1974

Ruperti, Alexander, *Cycles of Becoming,* California: CRCS 1978

On Psychology:

Assagioli, Roberto, *Psychosynthesis,* New York: Viking Penguin 1965

Maslow, Abraham, *Towards a Psychology of Being,* Kentucky: Litton Educational Publishers 1968

Rogers, Carl, *On Becoming a Person,* Massachusetts: Houghton Mifflin Co. 1961

Rosenblatt, Daniel, *The Gestalt Therapy Primer,* New York: Harper and Row 1975

Perls, Fritz, *Gestalt Therapy Verbatim,* New York: Bantam Books 1969

On Color

Anderson, Mary, *Colour Healing*, Maine: Weiser 1975

Birren Faber, *Color Psychology and Therapy*, New York: University Books 1961

Clark, Linda and Martine, Yvonne, *Health, Youth and Beauty Through Color and Breathing*, California: Celestial Arts 1976

Graham, F. Lanier, *The Rainbow Book*, Massachusetts: Shambhala publications 1975

On Astrology in General:

Arroyo, Stephen, *Astrology, Karma and Transformation*, Washington: CRCS 1978

Arroyo, Stephen, *Astrology, Psychology, and the Four Elements*, Washington: CRCS 1976

Crossley, Patricia, *Let's Learn Astrology*, New York: Exposition Press 1973

Davison, Ronald, *Astrology*, New York: Arco 1963

Green, Landis, *The Astrologer's Manual*, New York: Arco 1975

Parker, Julia and Derek, *The Compleat Astrologer*, New York: Bantam Books 1971